Jessica's Journey

By Carol Lee Ramie

CreateSpace Publishers
Scotts Valley, CA 95066

JESSICA'S JOURNEY

Copyright Carol Lee Ramie, 2014

CreateSpace Publishers
Scotts Valley, CA 95066

ISBN-13: 978-0615888521
ISBN-10: 0615888526

All photos by Carol Lee Ramie

Manufactured in the United States of America
First printing March 2014

DEDICATION

To Jessica

An Angel in the book of life wrote down Athena's birth,
Then whispered as she closed the book,
"Too beautiful for Earth"
– Unknown

ACKNOWLEDEGMENTS

To my husband Ron. Thank you for your unwavering, steadfast love. Life took our family to a place where none of us wanted to be. Your loving kindness and rock solid foundation in Christ, kept us together, at a time when we easily could have crumbled. My heart always has, and always will belong to you.

To my daughter Kendra and son Matthew. It's been a privilege to be the mother of such kind and compassionate children. Thank you for loving me through the hardest time of our lives. To my step-daughter Lisa, thank you for all that you do for our family. You are there in a heartbeat when any of us need you and I love you for that. To my daughter-in-law, Olivia – thank you for your beautiful remembrances of Athena, the photo book with her pictures, the engraved Christmas ornaments with her name and all of the other special things you did to help keep her close to us.

To my sister and best friend Gloria, my "Wilson." Your love kept my heart beating on the days when I felt I couldn't go on. I don't know how I could have made it without you... To my first love, my mother. Thank you for opening up your beautiful condo for us to stay in while in California. To my brothers Steve and Jimmy, thank you for your help and being there for Jess, CJ and me.

To Dr. Hirata, of the Fetal Diagnostic Institute of the Pacific, to OB/GYN doctor, Dr. Susan Chapman of Pali Women's Health Center, renowned heart surgeon of Stanford University of Medicine, Dr. Frank Hanley, the nurses of Lucille Packard Children's Hospital and countless other people who cared for Jessica and Athena, my deepest – deepest gratitude. To the employees and volunteers of the Ronald McDonald House in Palo Alto, California, especially "Joe" I will never forget you.

To our many friends who walked along side of us, Pastor Keith Ryder and Pastor James Anderson of Light of Promise Ministries, Deacon Mel Kalahiki who helped us bring Athena home and with her funeral – my heartfelt appreciation. To Pastor and Mrs. Goodale, of Koolau Baptist Church and Academy. It has been a privilege to know such virtuous people. You have both been such positive role models in Jessica's life and words can't express my gratefulness.

To my dearest friends Sheree and Geri – your friendship nourished me. To my swim buddies at the Kaneohe District Pool, especially Sam and lifeguard Chris, our fun talks in between swimming laps helped ease my weary soul. To Jessica's friends, Mailah, Rayna, Joanne and especially "Melly," I have learned how best friends can sustain you through the darkest of days. Thank you for loving Jessica and being the beautiful, kindhearted, devoted young women that you are.

To Rob Bignell and my dearest Norman Kaui, thank you for going on this journey with me and bringing honor to Athena's life with this book.

To my beloved dog, Zoë, who at 16 and in failing health – thank you for waiting for my return home before passing. This has been the first time I've written without you by my feet and I miss you terribly. I just know that you are with Athena in Heaven.

And lastly, to my daughter Jessica, thank you for giving me the precious gift of my granddaughter, Athena. I'll love her forever, I'll like her for always, as long as I'm living, her grandma I'll be....

Table of Contents

Jessica's Journey   1
The Beginning   3
August Journal Entry   17
A Day in September   21
Jessica Moves Back Home   23
Another September Day   25
September 18 Journal Entry   29
Another September Day Journal Entry   33
Present Day Reflections   39
A Week Before We Leave   43
A Few Days Before We Leave for California   45
October 19: The Day We Leave for California   47
Athena is Born   83
Athena is Released to the Ronald McDonald House   103
Athena Falls Ill   117
Afterword   127

Jessica's Journey

I've been told that eventually I will stop waking up in the middle of the night, tossing and turning, in turmoil. Lying there thinking about that night, watching my granddaughter in the panicked emergency room of a large national hospital in Northern California, as a swarm of doctors administered CPR compressions to her tiny chest. I've too been told that in time, the memories of my daughter, waiting outside of that packed and frenzied room, while she didn't have the slightest clue that her baby's life was leaving her, will also fade away. These agonizing images keep revolving in my mind like a slide show, image after image – and I'm unable to turn off the projector. When I think of one of the doctors walking Jessica down that long sterile, fluorescent lit hallway into a room that looked more like an interrogation area rather than a hospital, asking her to sit down then telling her the words that no mother should ever have to hear: "I'm sorry, but your baby has passed away," I feel trapped in my mind with no way out.

The unbearable feeling of standing next to my daughter as she slumped down and wept over the body of her three-week-old infant daughter, of refusing to leave the room – then standing at the opened door and, taking that one long last lingering look of the baby she rallied so hard to have and so desperately loved. I swear I could have died that night, doing anything to escape the excruciating anguish of her pain. I don't know when or how that image could ever dissipate. I don't care what anyone tells me...that memory and that memory alone will go with me to my grave.

Right now, these memories are raw and painful. The despair I feel of losing my grandchild is multiplied a million times over as I bear witness to my daughter's grief of losing her child. No mother should ever have to lose a child, and no grandmother, her daughter's baby.

From the time our children are born up until the time we mothers take our last breaths, our most meaningful occupation in life is to love and protect our children. Even though I know deep down inside that I could not have prevented this from happening, I wrestle with the "what ifs." If only we had taken the baby to the doctor the day before, if only we had taken her back to the miraculous hospital where Athena was born and underwent her incredible heart surgery If only, if only, if only....

It's been so long that we've been on this long and winding, miraculous yet heartbreaking journey that ended so tragically. Although I was by her side every step of the way, attending most all of her doctor appointments, relocating to another state for Jessica to bring her baby into the world, getting to know Athena long before she was born, watching her birth, and being there the moment she died...even though I lived and breathed it by her side, this was Jessica's Journey.

The Beginning

"I'm pregnant," Jessica told me on April 5. With no time to think and only react, the words of almost every parent of a young, unmarried daughter popped out of my mouth: "You're kidding, right?" I sat there in front of my computer screen at work, stunned, and the document I was working on disappeared before me. Jess, with her legs dangling as she sat on top another desk in my home office, awaited my delayed reaction to her shocking and unexpected announcement. As I sat there unable to speak, she just stared at me in silence, smiling. I wasn't sure what that smile was about. Was it from her own shock, guilt, happiness or nerves? I sat there dazed and confused waiting for the words, "I'm only kidding" to pop out of her mouth, but they never did.

Jessica had been going off and on with CJ, her boyfriend since the fifth grade, and now at 22, I was rather surprised that they were still together and taken aback that having a baby was in their plans. CJ was a nice boy, handsome, a year-and-a-half younger than she, but he loved his young life and probably didn't consider himself ready for fatherhood, just as he should not have been.

After a few moments with those words "I'm pregnant" whirling around in my mind like a level ten tornado, I snapped back to reality and asked her what she was going to do. The feelings of doubt and disappointment soon set in, and my spirit spiraled.

Jessica had been a typical all-American girl, going to a small private school, loving and excelling in sports, and possessing wonderful, sweet, spirited girlfriends whom I adored. She spent her high school summers at a prestigious summer camp, accompanied by her sister, who was just one year older than she. There they learned the outdoor skills that I never acquired as a child. To this day, I have never gone camping with my children, due to my ridiculous fear of bugs. They hiked, camped in the forest, and learned how to make a campfire with the materials that only nature provided. They were taught how to sail and were purposefully tipped over in the ocean while on a sailboat to learn how to deal with a capsized vessel and survival skills. They could put up an entire camp of tents and outdoor equipment at their high school retreats while the boys just sat there in awe watching them. As she grew older, she graduated to more extreme interest – skydiving! Of all the many adjectives that I could use to describe Jessica, "adventurous" took first place.

I drove Jessica and her sister to and from school just about every day of their childhood up until the last day of their senior years. I baked all of the holiday cookies and cupcakes from scratch for their school parties. I loved being their mother and was proud of the fact that I was happily married for 33 years to their father. We had lived in the same house since all three of our children had been born, and there was much stability in our lives. The thought of my daughter having her first child, under these circumstances, just didn't compute in my head. Call me naïve, but I just never saw this coming.

My brain eventually eased out of its stupor and reminded me that our children's actions are not always a reflection of their parenting. You can be utterly devoted and do everything in your power to see that your children take all of the right paths in life, but they still are their own person and will make their own choices. I had experienced much adversity in my own young life but grew up with a strong will and determination to make anything and everything work out for the better. Jessica inherited this same stamina of mine, and I knew that no matter what I said at that point, in her mind she already had a plan.

Just as a person says that their life flashes before them as they go through a near death experience, so many thoughts ran through my mind after she announced her news. My husband and I were still running a high profile company of 30 years at full throttle, and retirement was something we were striving towards. I suddenly felt a slight sense of panic when I thought about the possibility of Jessica deciding to raise this baby in our home.

Ron and I hadn't much time together during all these crazy busy years of running our company and raising our children. Although our son was grown and married with a family of his own, both of our daughters were still living with us. I was somehow looking forward to the day when it would be just he and I, in this home that we lived in for 30 plus years, anticipating our long-awaited and often talked about "golden years"; being able to do what we wanted, when we wanted to without worrying about the kids; a sandwich or cereal for dinner if we pleased; enjoying the peace and quiet we went without for what seemed like a lifetime. The thought of a baby in our home and the added responsibility scared me...yet somehow excited me at the same time. The notion of either one of my daughters having a baby while living at home was something that had never ever crossed my mind.

Not more than ten minutes after Jessica dealt me this un-expected news, I received a phone call from the pastor of our church informing me that one of our good friends, Craig, who had congestive heart failure, had just passed away. We had become especially close to this family, and with a heavy heart I immediately called my husband. He said he'd come right home so that we could meet with other members of our church at Craig's house, to be of comfort to his wife, who after 32 years now held the brand new title of widow.

Not expecting her dad to be home from work until the late afternoon, Jess said, "Are you going to tell him?" "No, you are, I said." Jess had absolutely nothing to fear as I knew without a shadow of a doubt that although Ron wouldn't be thrilled about it, he certainly would not be angry. Ron was an easy-going, loving, forgiving human being whom didn't jump to conclusions or judge anyone. Like the old saying, "If life hands you a bunch of lemons, make lemonade." Ron could have made enough lemonade to quench the thirst of a country. He was just that kind of guy.

Not long after we talked on the phone, Ron walked through the door. Jessica's eyes immediately locked with mine as he closed the screen door behind him. I looked at my husband and felt a sense of sadness, knowing that these were the last few moments of his life before he was hit with the big news that would change our lives forever.

He glanced at Jessica while her eyes met with mine, still wearing that same smile on her face. He stood there for a second with a look of perplexity and asked what was going on. In a hurry to get it over with, and without hesitation, she blurted out, "I'm pregnant!"

His reaction was exactly as I anticipated. Gentle and gracious. After asking her a couple of questions, mainly about how she was feeling and not what she was going to do, I grabbed my purse, and off we went to Craig's house to be with our beloved and brokenhearted friend, Margaret.

As we sat in the living room of Margaret's home, while people took turns spending time with Craig before the mortuary took his body away, I talked with some of my friends who also gathered there.

I can't quite remember everything we talked about as my emotions were all over the place. Having your daughter tell you she was pregnant and having a good friend dying on the same day was just too much to take in. I actually felt a disconnect from my body as I sat there. Our pastor's own daughter had a child out of marriage, and his wife reassured me that everything would be okay. I just couldn't comprehend this new equation in our life and felt tremendous anxiety wondering how in the world all of this would unfold. Jessica definitely loved the father of her child, but I knew deep down inside that most likely she would be raising the baby in our home.

The next couple of months passed by quickly. I kept waiting for her belly to grow as most of the time I forgot that she was pregnant. I kept asking her if she felt any signs of life, explaining to her how it might be a little hard to detect at first but that it would feel something like butterflies in her stomach. I can still remember my sister, when I was pregnant with my first child, telling me about the "butterflies" and here I was, sharing her story with my daughter. I just couldn't wait for that moment when she first felt her baby. I loved being pregnant and was anxious for her to experience, in my eyes, the most miraculous feeling in the world that only we women are privileged to experience: life growing within us.

On June 2, Jessica told me that she thought she felt "something." After asking her a few questions, we quickly concluded that she was feeling the first movements of her baby. I was ecstatic with this revelation and remembered when I first felt the "flutters" of my son within me. It was incredible to think that my daughter, my youngest child, was now experiencing this same feeling.

The next day, on my mother's 85th birthday, Jess sat at the top of the stairs that leads down to my home office and told me that she felt sick. The over-the-top fear that I feel when my kids are sick, I am certain, was a learned and irrevocable behavior of mine. My mom lost her mother when she was young, and she blamed it on an infection and the lack of penicillin in those days. She therefore had become a moderate germaphobe. Unfortunately that transference of worry rubbed off on me as I always felt extremely nervous when my children got sick. As soon as Jess told me she'd been ill since the day before I went into high alert. I asked her to make a doctor's appointment and to weigh herself so that we could start tracking her weight.

I will never forget that day. Not only did I profoundly love my daughter, but I now felt a deep sense of love and protectiveness for this unborn grandchild of mine. Jessica made an appointment while I made her some Ramen noodles, and all was well in both of our worlds.

Time passed and we remained as busy as ever with work, church and home life. I also swam a mile in the morning, several days a week, which added to the busyness of my days. Life was feeling almost normal again, and that felt good. Not long after, Jessica decided that she and CJ were going to try to make a go of it together and planned to move into his parent's house, in the little room downstairs, next to the garage. Seeing her leave pained me, as I believed that CJ wasn't ready to handle the responsibility that came along with her pregnancy. But this is what Jessica wanted – to be with the love of her life and to have this child with him. I knew he cared about her, but I also knew that this was overwhelming to him and that he honestly wasn't ready to settle into this position. I have said all along that I never faulted him for his feelings as he was young and didn't yet have much of life experience under his belt.

I knew he wouldn't be able to look after Jessica the way that she needed to be as her pregnancy progressed. I was so sensitive of my children's needs, and it was hard to see her go. Not so much for me, but for her. I was becoming overly concerned with her life and now in looking back, I wonder if it was an innate premonition. Little did I know then how my life would become completely immersed with hers when we eventually learned the news about the baby.

On June 28, Jess came home to gather the last of her things. While she was packing, she casually told me that she felt the baby really moving now. How much heartache could I take in a day? My daughter tells me that the baby is moving while she's finalizing her exit from our home? I felt tremendously sad, as I knew the path she was on was a rocky one, and no mother wishes this for her daughter, especially when she is with child.

The home she was moving into was close by, and not across an ocean like I did when I first left my parents. It was simply the fact that at a time when I thought she needed my help, and when I needed to mother her the most, she was moving into an environment that was not ours.

The entire situation would have been different had she been married and didn't have to worry about finances or working. But she was a nurturer and the caretaker of both her and CJ, and she now needed him to put her first. I had been blessed to be married to a loving man, a wonderful provider, who prepared a way for me to stay home when our first child was born. It wasn't easy, but we somehow worked it out.

After Jessica left home that day, I went into her nearly emptied bedroom and cried. Even though I was behind at work with so much to do, I stopped what I was doing just to take this all in and to think about what was happening. Her bedroom had an attached bathroom, and for some reason I started scrubbing the tub. I don't even know why I did it but most likely it was to work off the anxiety I was feeling. As I bent over scrubbing the tub with my rubber gloves on, I had to keep wiping the tears that streamed down my cheeks with my forearm, careful of not getting Ajax in my eyes.

I thought about how this very same bedroom and bathroom once belonged to my husband and me years before we renovated our home and adding a new master bedroom. This was the same bathroom that I took my pregnancy test when I learned I was pregnant with her! This is where she took her first pregnancy test, she later told me, before she confirmed it at the doctor's office. My lament, this day, was not just about her leaving home but more about my children growing up and letting go of their childhoods.

Jessica's sister was just a year older than she, and to me they felt like twins while raising them. I had been fortunate that my husband and I ran our own company when all three of my babies were born. When my kids were sick, I could bring them to work which is a privilege most women aren't afforded. Our roles were so interchangeable, always working together as a team. We were a close family, spending all of our free time with them. Our son played baseball for many years, and our girls grew up around the ballpark. We made wonderful friends there, had the best potlucks ever and got to spend a lot of quality time with our children. We never required "time away from the kids" that all the professionals tell you is so important for a relationship. We profoundly loved our children and always wanted to be with them. The only time our girls were away from us was at summer camp, which they couldn't wait to attend. The base for that camp was within two miles from our home, so even while away they were never far from us. The same went for our son. He traveled quite a bit during summer with various baseball teams but that was about it. We were always together.

Later in the day, I called Jessica to ask how she was doing and if I could move the remainder of her things out of her room so that her sister could move into it. Kendra had the smaller of the two bedrooms with no bathroom and was anxious to move into her room. "Can you give me just a week before letting her move in – to make sure this is all okay?" she asked. At that moment, I knew it was just as hard for her making the move from our house to CJ's as it was for me to see her go. I told her I would, but I knew she wouldn't be back. She was determined to make her relationship with CJ work. She wanted that "happy family" and would do everything in her power to make it happen.

To feel Athena kick for the first time is engraved in my mind forever. Jessica stopped by the house one morning for some rest and relaxation and to just hang out on the couch. These were the times when I felt exceedingly grateful for having a home office after 29 years of working in a building downtown. Jessica lay on the couch watching her favorite program, "The Price is Right," while I slipped into the kitchen to make one of her favorite breakfast of homemade waffles. "Come quick!" she blurted. She told me the baby was kicking and reached out for my hand and placed it on her now protruding belly. For the very first time, I felt the life of my granddaughter moving within her.

As I laid my hand on her belly, my joy was short lived, as it was soon replaced by the overwhelming worry over what we had just learned about the baby. I will never forget that day and I would give anything to be able to go back in time, to feel her kick once again.

On July 2, Ron and I were shopping at Costco, our cart filled to the top, when my cell phone rang. Before I answered, I glanced down and saw on the caller ID that it was Jess. I instantly knew something was wrong just by her calling me at that time of day and the sound of her voice. I could tell that she had been crying, and it takes a whole lot to make that girl cry.

She told me that she went in for a routine checkup, and a staff member at the Fetal Diagnostics Institute of Pacific told her about another test she could take, which was neither part of the regular check nor covered by her insurance. Normally, because of her young age, this test was not required. Jessica was very conscientious about money, and I was proud of the way she already handled the financial aspect of her pregnancy. She has signed up for a program with her employer, to have extra money taken out of her paycheck every two weeks to pay for the remaining fees that her insurance would not cover for her care during her pregnancy and the delivery of her baby. Even though this test wasn't covered by her insurance, Jessica wanted to have it done only because she wanted to see pictures of her baby. I have no doubt in my mind that God had His hand in her decision-making at that moment. The absence of this test could have proven to be terribly critical, and I believe it was a miracle that she chose to have it done.

Here she was, expecting to walk out of the clinic with photos of her beloved baby, but instead while conducting this high tech ultrasound, the doctor said it appeared that there might be something wrong with the baby's heart! Jess said that she needed to go to another clinic right away to be seen by another doctor who specialized in fetal medicine. We quickly moved to the cashier, loaded our groceries into the car and raced back home where she was to meet us so that we could drive her there. My husband and I barely spoke to one another while we quickly carried the groceries upstairs. We put all of the cold items into the refrigerator and left everything else out on the kitchen counter.

The 25-minute trip to the doctor's office was intense, and I knew that my husband was worried by the speed in which he drove. I looked in the review mirror at Jessica, sitting in the backseat, with her nose red from crying. She was busy texting CJ while my husband and I sat there in silence. Now that her pregnancy was starting to resonate with us, and our emotions were getting back to normal, now this? I tried my best to reassure her that everything would be okay but she didn't say anything back.

Jessica checked in with the receptionist, and we sat there anxiously waiting for her name to be called. The minutes dragged on, and she was finally summoned back into the examination room where the lights were dimmed and another 3D ultrasound was conducted. Ron and I sat next to her in the darkened room while we watched the images of her baby on the monitor, not knowing what we were really looking at.

The doctor studied the images of the baby's heart for quite some time and said that it looked like the baby had a rare condition known as Transposition of the Great Arteries, which is a major and critical heart defect. The two main arteries, the pulmonary and the aorta, were in the wrong position and would most likely have to be repositioned by open heart surgery after she was born. The only problem was is that there were no doctors in Hawaii who performed this type of surgery. We would have to fly to California for the delivery and for the surgical switch to be done right afterward. We also were told that this was a condition that was only seen in Hawaii once or twice a year and across the country, about 40 times. Dr. Hirata said that we needed to come back for further testing in four weeks to examine the baby's heart once it was larger. Jessica also had an amniocentesis done while we were there to check for gene abnormality. Ron and I sat next to her while the doctor pushed a long needle into her belly to extract amniotic fluid. That was especially hard to watch, but Jessica did well and after the needle was removed she blurted, "That wasn't so bad!" That was my Jessica, the bravest of the brave, and we all smiled in unison.

After her appointment was over, we drove back home in a state of disbelief. I can't even remember if Jessica came to our house afterwards or if we dropped her off at CJ's. After this day, nothing would be the same for any of us. Our days were filled with worry as we researched the baby's condition, Transposition of the Great Arteries on the Internet.

From that day on, my sleep changed dramatically having one restless night after another. I couldn't believe that this unborn child, so safe in her mother's womb, loved by us all, would have to face this brutal, life-threatening heart surgery after she entered the world. Why, dear God is this happening? This is just not the way it was supposed to be. I was grief-stricken over what might be before my daughter. At a time when she was supposed to be relishing her pregnancy, looking at baby books and putting together her nursery, we were all on the computer relentlessly studying this heart condition over and over again.

I became concerned with Jessica's lack of weight gain, but I knew it was from her worrying. I started to bring some of her favorite meals over to her now and then hoping to reassure her with my love and to get her to put some weight on. I missed having both of my daughter's at home together, and I now missed the old things I used to worry about. Jessica and the baby consumed my thoughts most of my waking hours, and I had a hard time concentrating at work, which in the world of investigations, demanded my full attention.

Jessica had another doctor appointment, on July 26, with the same doctor who initially diagnosed the baby with Transposition of the Great Arteries. We were anxious to see him as the baby's heart was four weeks larger, and he would better able to study it. I had been praying all the while that this was a misdiagnosis and that everything would be okay. But Dr. Hirada confirmed that the baby indeed had Transposition of the Great Arteries and would need to have the surgery. He referred us to a specialized pediatric cardiologist in Honolulu to have him to look at her heart as well. This doctor also would be the baby's physician after her surgery was completed and we returned home to Hawaii.

We subsequently met with this medical doctor a few weeks later as instructed. CJ's mom and grandmother, "Tutu", joined Jessica and I at the local children's hospital, and we didn't talk much as we waited for Jessica to be seen. We all squeezed around the table that Jessica lay on while the doctor pensively studied the images of the baby's heart on the monitor by ultrasound. I know everyone, including friends and family members, always had the best of intentions, but this was my daughter, and it's completely different when it's your own child. I was just as concerned about Jessica's well-being as I was with the baby's. These appointments were hard on Jessica, but she would never show her emotions nor would she ever cry. As her mother, I knew exactly what she was feeling and bore the brunt of her unspoken angst.

We stood there for the longest time, holding our breath, while waiting for him to say something. He studied image after image in silence. Inside I felt like screaming, "Why are you making us wait so long – SAY SOMETHING! Don't you know this feels like life and death to us?" When he finally spoke, he said that it might not be Transposition of the Great Arteries after all. "Oh my God!" All of our eyes silently met, and we crossed our fingers and once again held our breath as he continued to study the images...hoping, praying. My mind raced with thoughts of us resuming a normal life, a normal delivery, a normal baby, not having to leave our home, not having to travel to an unfamiliar place, not having to see my daughter suffer any longer, not having to see the baby undergo such a traumatic surgery. I was rudely snapped back into reality when he said, "No, I take that back, Dr. Hirata's diagnosis is correct. This is Transposition of the Great Arteries." I wanted to fall on the floor, I felt so despondent. My mind screamed, "Why did you say anything at all and get our hopes up? You should have said nothing!" I was so angry with his lack of bedside manners and it was difficult staying in control. How can this be true? Why Jessica, dear God, why? My poor daughter. I don't want this happening to her. Please let this be over!

During this visit and our previous appointments with other doctors, Jessica would not cry, which worried me. My two girls were such opposites. One displayed her emotions so openly while Jessica wouldn't let on to what bothered her, even in the direst of circumstances.

We discussed which hospitals the surgery could be performed at. At that point, we were looking at the University of California San Francisco, which would have been helpful to me as my mom owned a condo about 45 minutes away that she only lived in part of the year. Not only would we have a place to stay and save thousands of dollars on hotels, but we'd have the love and support of my family while we were so far away from our home in Hawaii. It wasn't decided yet which facility we would be sent to, but we would be notified once that decision had been made. I subsequently spent so much time on the Internet studying the different locations on Google maps, looking at the medical facilities, freeways and travel routes. I still couldn't believe I would soon be relocating there with my daughter.

The enormity of our situation started sinking in soon after this appointment. I started seeing pregnant women everywhere I went and, sad to say, I started feeling angry, so very angry, wondering how in the world something like this could happen to my daughter, to our family. Hadn't we been through enough already? I had almost lost my husband to a brain aneurysm years before and that was a traumatic event that took so much out of me and my children. Why did we have to go through another serious blow like this again?

I started feeling disheartened, and although I continued on with all of my normal activities, all that I felt like doing was lying in bed and watching TV. I was exhausted. But I didn't. I just couldn't as I didn't have the time. I had to be strong for my daughter, and I could not let her down for a minute.

Just about this time, I started keeping a hard cover journal for the first time since I'd been a teenager, and I am grateful that I did. It was filled with writings about our lives before Athena was born and when we were filled with HOPE.

I took it everywhere I went, doctor's appointments, on the

plane, in waiting rooms, in my bedroom. I'd sit there with my journal on my lap, writing while fetal monitor belts were hooked up around Jessica's stomach, tracking the heartbeat of Athena. I find myself reading the entries often, slipping back into the days that even when I felt frightened and overwhelmed, I felt optimistic. Never once did I ever think we'd lose her, especially after the remarkable way she came into the world.

August Journal Entry

I am having a really hard time today. I feel so anxious that I can barely concentrate at work or much of anything else. Even though I hate medication and will only take a Tylenol at the last resort, I'm thinking about seeing my doctor about the constant, relentless anxiety that I can't seem to shake. When my thoughts start wandering on how I will be able to manage all that is before me I often have heart palpitations. I honestly don't know how I will be able to do this. Preparing for our trip, getting others in place to take over my position during my absence, leaving my company. Shipping my car to California and driving in a state that has "real freeways" compared to what we drive on in Hawaii. Although I've always been a strong and independent woman, I've had my husband's reassurance in tough situations. I now was going to be without him at a time when I needed him the most.

CJ would also be traveling to the mainland with us. I not only felt an enormous responsibility for my daughter, but I also felt responsible for his welfare as well. What seemed to constantly concern me was the thought of driving there. How would it feel to drive in a huge state that I wasn't familiar with? Where I didn't know where I was? I had heard so many stories about driving in California and the crazy freeways there. Hawaii has freeways, but compared to California they were more like "Disneyland" highways. I was aware that I am an "in control" person and that spills over into my needing to know where I am and where I am going at all times. The thought of driving and not being able to visualize the end destination felt particularly taxing to me – especially with my very pregnant daughter as my passenger.

Had it been just me, alone, driving there, well, the worry would not have been so great.

My car was equipped with GPS, and I would later become attached to the "voice" that directed us throughout our travels there. I purchased my car from a dealership in Texas a couple of years before, and had it transported to California then shipped to Hawaii. After it arrived here, and I started driving it, I found out that the GPS system didn't work in Hawaii. It had something to do with the software and satellites in the year that the car was manufactured. I was so disappointed and after exhausting all efforts of what I could do to get it to work, I threw the disk away. Once I decided that I would ship my car to California, I had to order the disc again. Whoever thought I'd need it?

During our commutes back and forth to Stanford before Athena was born, CJ and I would often crack up at the way the GPS pronounced words while guiding us to our destinations, with one of our favorite streets being Arboretum Road. Every time she would say it, CJ and I would cackle like parrots, mimicking her voice and laughing. As odd as it sounds, every once in a while, even though it didn't work in Hawaii, after we returned home, I'd put the disc in just to hear her voice. When I heard it, I'd let my mind wander back into time, to one of those moments when we felt joyful – before our hearts were broken.

I've been thinking about how we recently lost both our handyman for our home and our good friend Craig, and all the changes that have taken place in our lives. I then began reflecting on something one morning that I hadn't thought about in a long time.

About 14 years ago, my husband nearly died of a brain aneurysm and after nine hours of brain surgery, he made a miraculous recovery. I realized that part of my anxiety of our upcoming trip stemmed from the worry of something happening to him after I left. The fear him nearly dying had never completely left me and always lingered in the deepest part of my mind. To this day, whenever he gets a headache, I am on the alert and ask him the questions I know he is so tired of me asking, "Where is the pain? Is it behind your neck? Are you sure you are okay?" Now, not only being afraid for the baby, I started feeling uncomfortable with the thought of leaving my husband. After his aneurysm, I took on a lot more responsibility at our company, as well as in our lives in general, that I never was able to let go of. But that was par for my course. I was born a responsible child who became an even more responsible adult. We always joked that if you looked up the word "responsible" in the dictionary, my picture would be next to the definition.

I found myself starting to distance myself from Ron as I started mentally preparing for this challenge I faced without him and the worry I had of leaving him behind.

We had been waiting to find out if CJ would be able to make the trip to California with us. The Human Resource department of the company where he and Jessica both worked at was putting him through the ringer and they initially turned down his request for a family leave of absence. Both he and Jessica explained the situation to them both verbally and in writing and the company had to contact their corporate office to see if an exception could be made. How could they not make an exception under these circumstances? I found it astounding how regulations have to be so carefully followed nowadays even the direst of circumstances. What ever happened to the heart of the matter? We needed to be in California a month before Jessica gave birth. Then, after the baby had her heart surgery, we couldn't predict how long her recovery would take. At this point, we were thinking we would be gone two to three months, but how could we pinpoint it? There simply was no way to predict the amount of time we'd need to be away. It seemed like every time we turned around there was always a new battle to fight.

I was still unsure if I should ship my car to California. I had to weigh out the pros and cons and make so many decisions as I prepared for our travels. It would cost about $2400 to ship my car to California and back, which was just slightly more than if I were to have rented one. Still, in a place where everything would be unfamiliar, it would be some semblance of security to have my car. Like a comfortable pair of shoes or blue jeans, your car is simply your car.

I was just telling my husband that we need to try to incorporate some joy into our lives as it seems that we've lost our way with each other since the news. I knew in light of what was going on it was understandable, but we just couldn't let ourselves be overcome by this situation.

I remember the week before Ron had his brain aneurysm. I was feeling upset and overwhelmed trying to balance my life with our company and our young children at the time. After his brain hemorrhage, I remember thinking how I would have given anything to go back to that week – to those set of problems when I thought my life was so hard. What we were now facing with a brain injury was a matter of life and death and everything else was meaningless.

I think about our new situation and wonder what our lives would be like today if we weren't planning on the birth and surgery of Jessica's baby, so far away from home. I think the hardest part of all of this is having to be in California when this all takes place. Maybe if it all could have happened in Hawaii, it wouldn't have felt so overwhelming.

To know that my daughter is struggling with her own emotions is more than I can take. She doesn't talk about it at all but I know she is worried beyond words.

In the middle of the night, I think about the baby whom Jessica and CJ have named Athena Marie. Before they knew what they were having, CJ told Jess that if they had a daughter, he wanted to name her Athena after the Greek goddess of wisdom and warfare – beautiful and strong like her mother. I have been writing a song for her and will find someone to lay down the tracks and record it at some point. I have written songs for all of my children, and "Athena's Song" came to me in my dreams as all the rest of them did, in bits and pieces, until it all fell into one beautiful place.

A Day in September

This has been one of the harder weeks of my life. In all honestly, the only event that has surpassed this was the week of Ron's brain aneurysm.

We had an unbelievable experience with Jessica's medical insurance. The large national company that she works for had changed health care networks, and Jessica was never notified. All of the doctors that she had been seeing up until this point were not covered under her new plan. We had been working with a team of physicians and coordinators to transfer Jessica's care to Stanford Hospital in Palo Alto, California, and we were told that not only were her previous visits not covered under her new plan, but we were going to have to start over and put a whole new team in place with only six weeks before we were scheduled to leave. This was absolutely horrifying! Jessica and I were both on the phone for two days straight pleading with everyone that we spoke to, telling them that this just can't happen with such little time before we had to leave. Jessica also called me to say that things weren't working out between her and CJ and that she wanted move back home.

Jessica Moves Back Home

J essica moved back home today. We picked her up at 6:30 a.m., at CJ's. When we pulled up to the house, she was standing outside on the street with her face reddened from crying...I felt frozen. There she stood, looking more like 15 than 22, carrying a baby that needed heart surgery, and now broken up with the father of her child. My all-American girl, with an all-American life, loved by the same two parents, living in the same home her entire life, now facing problems and heartache that neither my husband nor I could help fix. Nothing seemed to be going right in her life and she was devastated. Her pain was my pain, and I could barely withstand it. I wanted out from my life, but that was just selfishness speaking. So we continued on.

I called her doctor's office today and asked if they could take Jess off of work and place her on temporary disability. Jessica was determined to work until the day before we had to leave for California to save money for her long leave of absence. But I could no longer watch her continue on like this, and I put my foot down – insisting that she stop working. She is an amazing young woman – such a hard worker, never missing a day of work unless an emergency occurred. Even with the countless doctor appointments she had to attend, she made sure to always be at work on time. She needed rest, not just physical rest but emotional rest. How much pressure could she take? I worry about the baby inside of her and what she must be feeling with all that Jess is going through.

Tonight, Jessica, her sister Kendra, Ron and I all sat in the living room watching a movie together, something we didn't do too often. We had some dinner, and Athena started to get active around her usual time of 7:30. I laid my hand on Jessica's stomach once again to feel her kicking and moving about. So very tenderly Ron felt Athena move for the first time tonight, and Kendra did, too! Jessica and Kendra had been apart for a while, and tonight their connection seemed strengthened, and my heart felt content. I made us all orange juice and vanilla milkshakes before watching the movie. I've been busy trying to get some extra calories into Jessica's diet, as she hadn't gained enough weight. So as she gains weight, we do, too! I feel so blessed tonight and thank God for answering my prayers for family unity. My sister and good friend Sheree had been committed to praying for our family, and with their prayers combined with those of many others, including mine, I see God moving in our home.

Jessica and I leave on our journey in just 44 days. But what keeps us focused in light of all that we have to do to prepare for our departure is we will return with Athena! How I already love her!

Another September Day

I am sitting in the lounge of the Infinity car dealership while my car is being serviced for its big sail across the sea. We are now just about a month out from our trip. My anxiety level has been quite high, and I realized that I should learn some breathing exercises as when I get anxious, my breathing gets shallow and my chest gets tight, which scares me.

Jessica is still home and is doing better. I am certain that she is more comfortable back at our home, her home, as she is once again able to move about the house in her favorite attire, barely dressed! She loves to walk around in her underwear! She has the body of an adolescent, which allows her to get away with it without being indecent. She has spent so much of her life in a swimsuit that it's a natural way for her to dress. I swear, at one time, she had more bikinis in her drawers that my husband had socks! Also, to have a bathroom close by is essential for her now. At CJ's, she had to leave his little room downstairs, walk outside and up to the main house to use the bathroom. At this point, with the baby pressing on her bladder, this was a hardship on her.

I am making milkshakes for her every day now, which she likes, and they are good for her. Full of protein and calories and she is finally gaining weight!

Last night we went to her brother's house to celebrate our grandson's 14th birthday. Jessica hadn't been feeling well all day and lay on the couch for the most part of the party. My son sat next to her and patiently rested his hand on her stomach waiting for Athena to move, and his eyes lit up when he felt her. My sweet, sweet boy – a sight to behold in a mother's eyes.

We left my son's house early that evening, and when we got home, Jessica asked me to give her a sinus treatment. She's had a problem with her allergies since she was a child, and I discovered a way to help alleviate her discomfort.

I helped her up on our 10-foot long kitchen counter, which she laid down on with a towel rolled up behind her neck. I grabbed a stack of washcloths from the kitchen drawer and wet them in the sink. I then put one in the microwave, warmed it up, and placed it on her face, from the nose up and applied pressure to her sinus areas with my fingers. As the cloth started cooling off, I was already warming up another one in the microwave. After about ten minutes of warm cloths and my therapeutic finger massage on her face, she started to feel better.

While her face was covered, I watched her belly for Athena to move, and I wasn't disappointed. I stood there with my hands on Jessica's covered face, while thinking about the baby inside her. Even though her belly was so big now, I still couldn't believe that my youngest child, my baby, was having a baby. A baby who, now safe in her womb, would be born into this world only to have her chest opened and her heart surgically repaired.

The picture was just simply wrong. I agonized all the time knowing what was ahead of my daughter and her beloved baby.

This past Monday, the worship leader from our church, Pastor Abraham, came to my house, and I introduced to him the song I had written for Athena. I played the melody on my piano, and he instantaneously picked it up on his guitar. I gave him a copy of the lyrics, and he recorded the melody of the song to take home with him so that he could work on it. He graciously granted my request to play and sing the song at Jessica's baby shower. I have not hinted or played a note of the song on my piano while Jess has been around, as I wanted it to be a complete surprise.

I know that she will love it and in light of our circumstances, it's so appropriate.

Athena Marie
There's a love, a new love in our lives,
Deep within, and she's right here inside,
A new branch, of our family tree,
Oh how we adore you, Athena Marie.
Won't be long, we'll be holding you tight,
Whispering – lullabies in the night,
Once you're here, we will never let go,
Athena, Athena, we love you so.
Our sunshine, that's what you are,
Bright as the first evening star,
With you now, it all feels so right,
And we will adore you for the rest of our lives.
There's a love, a new love in our lives,
A baby girl, we're so joyful inside,
Won't be long, till we all get to see,
Our brand new addition, Athena Marie,
Oh how we adore you, Athena Marie.
We will always love you, Athena Marie.

Pastor Abraham is one of the most musically gifted people I've known, and I have no doubt that the Heavens will open when he sings her song. I've also been putting together a slide show with all of Athena's ultrasound photos. Because her heart has to be closely monitored, Jessica has to go to the doctor often. After the images of her heart are taken the technicians take photos of her face just to help keep Jessica's spirits up. Every single time we've seen her, we have oohed and awed in unison. We've been getting to know what she looks like already, and it seems that she has her Daddy's nose!

My daughter Kendra, who is just a year older than Jessica, had been dating a young man who both Ron and I really liked and thought that this might be "the one." I was happy seeing Kendra falling in love and felt comforted in knowing that he'd be around to help both Kendra and Ron during my absence. Of all things a woman could adore about a future son-in-law, he cooks! Because we would be gone for

Thanksgiving, we made a Thanksgiving dinner on Jessica's birthday, in August, inviting our entire family to celebrate it with us. This amazing young man made the best mashed potatoes I'd ever tasted and moved about the kitchen with such confidence. When I found out that they had broken up, I felt yet another blow to our circumstances. I just wanted my family to be okay while I was gone. As most women, I certainly was the hub of our family and always kept things running at home in a very maternal manner. I knew both Ron and Kendra would definitely feel the void of my absence and it saddened me to leave them. We had so much uncertainty surrounding us and this just felt like another big setback.

September 18 Journal Entry

Tomorrow makes one month until we leave for our trip. It's hard to imagine that this is all going to take place, that we are really are going to do this. Our leaving continues to feel surreal and I just can't seem to surrender to this situation. Although I was born in the mainland I've lived in Hawaii for over 40 years and California was far from familiar territory anymore. I wondered when all of this would start feeling real to me as it somehow still felt like a dream. I kept trying to visualize it all taking place. Jessica's labor is now in full force in my mind with the worry twirling about like a baton. I can't believe that I will witness my daughter going through the most challenging passage of womanhood – childbirth – and I know I will have to be strong for both she and CJ. I keep trying to envision it, as if I'm practicing drills, to desensitize myself for when that time comes. I have been so strong all of my life, but this situation has brought me to my knees and unleashed fears I didn't know that I had.

Then we will have to endure the next big task at hand – the baby's open-heart surgery –and seeing her afterwards. It's going to be hard on Jessica, and I will have to be diligent about keeping my emotions in check for her. Again, I am rehearsing every day, so when it arrives, I will know what to do with my imaginary practice drills in place.

It seems that Jessica is only now starting to enjoy her pregnancy, and I am feeling more hopeful. Because of the circumstances, Jessica had not spoken much of the baby. I suspected it all along and later confirmed that she didn't speak of Athena out of her fear of losing her.

Last night, my daughter Kendra, Jessica and I did a full

belly casting of Jessica's stomach and chest. What a comical and lighthearted time that was! I hadn't seen my daughter's breast for some time and I was rather surprised at how "immodest" she was. Kendra and I placed layer upon layer of plaster of Paris, over her breast and belly, while she giggled, with plans on using the mold for an envelope card box at her baby shower. It was a messy project, but we all laughed a lot as we did it. The mold turned out sweet, and Jessica was pleased. It was good to have those moments where we forgot about the seriousness of her situation and did things that women were supposed to do during "normal" pregnancies.

I had started planning her baby shower long before we learned of the baby's heart problem, looking endlessly through shower themes and ideas. In between editing film or taking photographs of video footage to place into our investigative reports, I would hop on websites to look at ideas. When I wasn't working, my entire thought process was all about my daughter and her baby. At one point, Jessica started to waver on having a shower at all. It wasn't long before I took control and stood firm on the decision that we would have this shower and that was that. In my mind, never once did I think that the baby wouldn't make it, not after all that we learned about the surgery and the success rate of it. In Hawaii, the doctor said he sees about two cases of TGA a year and 40 cases nationally. He said that although those numbers seemed few – heart surgeons were now extremely advanced in their surgical skills – and that the physicians that would perform Athena's surgery were renown and accredited around the world. I just knew then that everything would be okay.

We eventually picked out the date of October 9th for the shower, which would only be ten days before we left for California. In the back of my mind I didn't know how I'd be able to pull all of this off. I had so much to do at work with the preparation of my absence. Also, my beloved poodle, of 16 years, Zoë, was in failing health. I knew she would be extremely distressed by my absence and feared she might not make it while I was away. I raised her from a puppy and we were together all of the time – both at home and at work. She was hard of hearing, couldn't see well, and her joints were affected by her age. But how I loved her! After I read the book, and saw the movie "Marley and Me," I was so moved by the story that I wrote an article titled "Zoë and Me," which was published in our local newspaper. I wrote about this beloved aging companion of mine. And, much like Marley's owners, I wondered what I would do without her. She was literally not more than three feet away from me at any given time of the day or night. Even when I took her to the dog park, while my other dog, little Sophia, romped around with the dogs, Zoë stayed right by me.

While sitting outside on our deck and drinking coffee in the morning, my husband and I would often look at the clouds and name the shapes we would see. Without fail I always saw white poodles. In my article, I said that when that day comes, when she is no longer with me, all that I will have to do is look at the clouds and I'll always be able to see her. I felt so awful about having to leave her but what could I to do?

My car was going to be shipped to the mainland around that same time as the baby shower, and I felt inundated by my things-to-do list. The chronic worry about what was before us was always in the back of my mind and left me feeling drained. I hired the father of Jessica's best friend, Melly, who is a chef by trade, to cater the food at the shower to help lighten the load. After searching long and hard through countless web sites I had discovered the theme, "A New Little Princess," which we coordinated the color theme around. Jessica and I stayed busy ordering party supplies over the Internet and stopping into party stores every chance we got, all while I was still running our company and tending to my family.

Jessica's sister and some of her best friends volunteered to help decorate the room that the party was to be in. I think our guest list was about 75 people and planning her shower helped keep my mind from dwelling on the nervousness that never seemed to leave me. I was exhausted all of the time, a type of exhaustion that was unfamiliar to me as I am naturally full of energy. I had never faced an enormous event such as this without my husband. Because we run a company together, it wasn't possible for us to both leave our company, so naturally it was me that would be with our daughter.

I had more to do than I'd ever been faced with, especially getting our company in place for my absence. My husband and I are responsible for totally different areas of the company we ran. I signed up to a computer service so that I could log into my computer at work to do what I could while in California. I spent endless hours of duplicating and packing software and backing up information to take with me. No matter how much I prepared, it never felt like enough. There was, however, a stroke of luck that came my way during this time. Kamaile, our administrative assistant who used to work with our company before she had children, committed herself to pitching in during my absence. She was a talented young woman who could do much of what I needed done while I was away. I felt extremely grateful for her dedicating her time to work for me while I was gone as it was a huge sacrifice for her to do so. I was the main editor at our company, proofing the final draft of all the investigations and this was one part of my job that I had to do while away no matter what. I also had to handle the financial aspect of the business, as there was no one else I trusted to do this. This is when working for someone else would have been a blessing. But I wouldn't trade working with my husband, at our own company, for the world.

Another September Day
Journal Entry

About a month before her baby shower, we took Jessica to the north side of the island to do a photo shoot for the invitations to her baby shower. Being part Hawaiian, her apparel that day fit her to a T – a bikini top and a pareo wrapped around the lower part of her body, with her large belly exposed. Her long, beautiful Hawaiian hair was draped over her shoulder with a plumeria flower tucked behind her ear. The day was light and joyful, and it was fun having the family together. Random people in the park stared at Jessica with smiles and admiration. I thought to myself, as I did in so many other situations, "If they only knew... if they only knew." Jessica's smiles for the camera that day somehow seemed forced but even in light of her worry, she was in love with her baby and it showed in the digital images captured of her. She was striking, being pregnant, so natural and exotic looking. Every time we attended a doctor appointment the receptionist and nurses always commented on how stunning she looked. Even the other pregnant women in the waiting rooms always took notice of her, and I'm sure, felt envious of her breathtaking beauty.

After the photo shoot was done, we stopped at a nearby 7-Eleven Store to buy some drinks. The weather was exceptionally muggy, and we hadn't brought any water with us. As the cashier was ringing up our beverages, and snacks she said to Jessica, "Honey, you look so beautiful, you are going to make all the young girls want to become pregnant!" I felt happy when she received those types of compliments.

With all that she was going through, she deserved something to raise her spirits. It struck me so odd how picturesque she looked on the outside in lieu of what was going on within her. I know she thought about the baby's condition constantly and she later admitted to me that CJ, too, was afraid of the baby dying.

During this entire time, Jessica continued working and I admired her determination in such a profound way. She was a master planner, just like her mama. She worked hard at being organized and prepared for every aspect of her life. But here she was...confronted with a situation so far out of her control. I can't imagine what went through her mind every day. Just what went through my mind was hard enough, and I'm certain her thoughts were beyond description.

Every spare moment I had was spent on making lists of all the things I needed to prepare for our company, the trip and putting the final touches on the baby shower. What an undertaking that was. I thank God for my mother's good genes as I have been blessed with stamina and discipline. No matter how hard things get, I was always able to get whatever needed to be done, done. In the privacy of my office, I'd often experience short crying jags to release the relentless stress I was under. Planning a large shower on top of leaving for our trip, all within 10 days of both events – looking back, well, I just don't know how I did it.

The baby shower was beautiful. We'd always referred to Jessica as "the princess," and the theme "The New Little Princess" was therefore perfect. Any little girl of my daughter would become heir to her royal princess hood! Because we would be so far away from home when the baby was born and our friends and relatives would be unable to see Athena when she arrived, we elected to have a co-ed shower, so that all of those closest to us could celebrate this time together before our big Aloha!

Several women from my church volunteered to help with the decorations and the amazing games that even the men had fun participating in. The color theme of the shower decorations was pink, white and green. The party plates had little crowns on them, and the tables were littered with small pacifiers, baby bottles, rattles and little candy boxes with miniature crowns. The center pieces were huge pink baby bottles with a bouquet of balloons attached to each one, filled with at least 75 pieces of candy. Jessica helped with everything every step of the way. You would have never guessed she was pregnant by the graceful way she moved. She never complained about much of anything, which concerned me, too.

The highlight of the day was when Pastor Abraham sang Athena's song. I was so nervous while waiting for him to show up that my hands were actually shaking. He was supposed to be there at 1 p.m., and once it was 1:10 p.m., I called him on his cell phone. He said that he was having trouble finding our location, so I talked him to it while I stood in the parking lot watching for him. My knees felt weak when I saw him get out of his truck with his guitar in hand.

We called everyone inside the main party room and had Jessica and CJ sit down in the front. The expression on their faces was of bewilderment – wondering what in the world was going on. This was the moment I had been looking so forward to. I have written songs for all of my children, and now, I'd written a song for my daughter's baby. Because of these incredible circumstances, the song had more meaning than any song I had ever written.

By the look on Jessica's face, I could tell she had no idea that I had done this. She and CJ both sat there in awe while he sang, and there wasn't a dry eye in the room. After he finished singing, Jessica got up and hugged me, and I felt a streak of contentment that I hadn't felt in a long, long while.

The day was beautiful with the sun out in all of its glory. Everyone who was there knew about the baby's condition, and I am certain no one had attended a baby shower quite like this one before. Even in the midst of the joy that day, the fact that Jessica was carrying a baby with a unique heart problem always lurked in the back of everyone's mind. Deep down inside, I am certain, everyone felt taken aback, knowing that his precious little life, once entering this wonderful world, instead of being born in the way that all babies should be – placed in their mother's arms – would be whisked away into the NICU unit without her mom even getting to hold her.

After the shower, and the long tiring process of cleaning up, Jessica and CJ spent some time together at our house, looking through all of the beautiful gifts and cards that they received. I sat down at my piano and played Athena's song for them, now being able to tell them all about it – how the lyrics and music came to me during the middle of many nights, how I worked on the song early in the mornings on my digital piano, with the volume turned down, while Jessica was asleep. They were both touched, and it was a perfect way to end the day by privately playing it for them. For the first time in a long, long while, I slept the entire night through.

I was relieved that the party was over and that the time had finally come so I could give my full attention to getting ready to leave my life here, my home, my husband, my other children, my grandchildren, and my dogs. The thought of leaving my job left me feeling fragmented. My husband depended heavily on me at work, and it seemed that no matter how much I prepared for my absence, the worry still lingered.

My mom said that my over the top worry was par for my course, reminding me as she had so many times before, that I was born being a responsible child – so much so that when I was 13, instead of being out with my friends doing foolish things, my cousin Julie and I were soliciting neighbors for odd jobs and made money by cleaning the yards of elderly widows.

Surrendering has never been a strong point of mine, and I wasn't about to change – not now – not quite yet.

From the time we learned about Athena's heart condition until the date of our departure to California, I couldn't even begin to estimate how many phone calls went back and forth to all the medical parties concerned. What went into Jessica's care with her upcoming transfer from Hawaii to Stanford University Medical Center, one of the world's leading research and teaching institutions located in California, was an undertaking I wouldn't wish upon anyone. There were so many people involved and even though most of them showed compassion for our situation, they had not a clue how it felt to be on our end of it. I constantly felt like I was teetering on the edge of a cliff, holding on for dear life. I didn't realize how difficult it was to transfer the care of a patient from one state to another. Everything was contingent upon something else, and time was narrowing down for our departure, without a doctor's appointment in place for Jessica once we arrived there.

Jessica had so many contractions during the last two months of her pregnancy it was unsettling. After the shower was over with we continued to see her OB/GYN and Jessica, even up to the day before we left for California, had regular contractions. She was hospitalized twice and administered medication to slow them down. She spent the last week before we left, on complete bed rest to prevent early labor. She was now placed on a daily dose of medicine that left her feeling nauseated and ill. The baby could not be born here, and I constantly worried about her contractions. I was one big ball of anxiety, and even though I had a few good friends that I could share my feelings with, there was nothing anyone could do to help. My sister – who also was my best friend – had just been diagnosed with breast cancer, and I hated burdening her with my problems, but oh how I needed her.

I spent so much time by Jessica's side, while she lay on the table in the doctor's office with a fetal monitor strapped around her belly. She usually spent her time lying there, not saying a word, texting on her phone, while I sat there watching the paper trickle out of the machine with the peaks and valleys of Athena's heartbeats.

I imagined the baby inside her and thought how peaceful and safe she was and thought what it was going to be like to see her, to hold her. I tried hard to keep up a strong front for my daughter, but I was filled with angst. I still couldn't wrap my brain around the fact that this baby was going to need heart surgery. It was like signing up and winning the unluckiest lottery in the world.

Athena was never very active when these readings were taken, and the nurses would always have to hold a buzzer next to Jessica's belly to wake her up to get her moving so that an accurate reading of her heart rate could be achieved.

During the 3D ultrasound pictures that were taken of Athena while in utero, and even in some pictures of her after she was born, you would often see her arms up against her ears. My guess was that she didn't like the sound of that God forsaken buzzer that she heard so many times and was probably trying to block it out by covering her ears! I think of Athena in the warm fluid within the amniotic sac, in a dream state, living, growing, and preparing to be born. Then suddenly out of nowhere, an unexpected sound of an obnoxious buzzer rocks her world, forcing her to wake up and give the nurses what they wanted – an accurate reading of her heart rate.

Present Day Reflections

A s I type these words today, I know that the hard part of this story is yet to come and there is a part of me that wants to "select all" and press the delete button to end this undertaking. I am not even sure at this point if I will even finish. I will soon have to face reliving the hard part all over again and I often question why I am writing this at all. Putting this into words often paralyzes me with sorrow and I just want to wilt away.

Today is the Fourth of August, and Athena died eight months ago. I am at work at I type with my secretary behind me. She can't see my face, and I am counting the minutes until she leaves. I want so much to lay my head down on my desk and cry. I can hardly contain myself today and just want to be alone. I know I am speaking for myself and other members of my family. We have some good days, some better days, some bad days, and then some terrible days. Today is one of the terrible days.

Someone once said to me after Athena died, and we had returned home to Hawaii, that it was probably best that she died so young so that we didn't get too attached to her. I don't think I will ever forget those words. This person is still my friend, and I never told her how much those words hurt. I have learned that people often say careless things when they don't know what else to say, so I never held it against her. I have learned that love cannot be measured in days, weeks, years or a lifetime. I loved Athena as much, if not more, than anyone else I have ever loved and will grieve for her for the rest of my life.

I went to the cemetery today to spend time with my beloved granddaughter. Athena is buried in one of the most beautiful cemeteries, I am certain, in the world. Jurassic Park like mountains surround this memorial park, and the grass is green twelve months out of the year. I find great solace at her gravesite. I cut the grass, rearrange the photos and other decorations on her grave, and weep when I am there. I saved many of the trinkets from her baby shower and lay them on her grave. I look back at those moments of decorating the party tables and fast-forward to placing the trinkets on her resting place. Who should ever have to do that? Who, God who?

All that I think about is this child that we rallied so hard to bring into this world, who survived this miraculous heart surgery, only to fall ill from something else. All of our hopes and dreams of loving her, of bringing her home, of watching her grow up – shattered.

I think of the last day she was alive, of how privileged I was to have spent the whole morning with her while Jessica, who was running on empty, asked if I could watch her while she slept a little longer. How fortunate I was to have had that last day with her. She had four grandparents, but I was the one who was blessed to have held her most and the last to hold her. The one, who got to sing to her, rock her, feed her, change her diaper. The one who got to kiss her and tell her how much I loved her over and over again.

I have been reading a book about a mother whose only child was arrested for murdering his wife's ex-husband, shooting him dead in cold blood. The son apparently was led to believe that this man was sexually abusing his stepdaughters and took the situation into his own hands. This book is about a mother's inexpressible grief of seeing her son, her only child, incarcerated for the rest of his natural life. The crux of the book was about grieving and how we can only get through it by totally surrendering to our situation.

I have tried my best to surrender to Athena's death but I can't. I've come to realize that because of my daughter's grief, that only a mother who has lost a child can know, I cannot let Jessica suffer alone. I have also learned that grandparent's grief is often overlooked by society in general. Not only do we grieve for the loss of our grandchild, but also we are left with the overwhelming heartache of watching our own child suffer.

A Week Before We Leave

The day we took my car down to the harbor for its big sail across the ocean had arrived, and it felt strange to set it off on its voyage without me. We had to go through a large checklist of things to do with the car before it could board the ship. My husband and I changed all the paperwork, including the title, into my name only, to avoid any hassle of it being in both of our names. The car had to be clean, inside and out, and even under its carriage.

My husband's brother works for the shipping company that transported my car to California. Vern met us at the harbor that day and assisted us on getting it on board. When I finally signed off on the paperwork and said goodbye to my car, I cried. This entire situation felt unreal to me most of the time but today it felt real and it felt scary. No turning back now. The next time I would see my black beauty would be in California. My husband and I walked away from the harbor, with his arm around my shoulder. He drove me home while I quietly sat there, thinking about the next part of our journey. I would be without my car for about ten days, but it would be there waiting for me once we got there. We were fortunate that we had an extra vehicle that we were going to sell but held off until my return home so that I would have something to drive while my car was shipped to and back from California.

A Few Days Before We Leave for California

J essica had been camping out in our living room since her doctor put her on complete bed rest to slow down her contractions. I always worried about the baby being born anywhere besides California, especially on the plane. I know there is a rule about flying when you are pregnant and that you are not allowed to fly after a certain number of weeks within your due date. I also worried that someone from the airline would question Jessica's pregnancy, but that was just me. If there was something to worry about, I'd worry about it.

Two days before we left, I walked into the living room, and there laid an open suitcase in the middle of the floor filled with everything she was taking for the baby. For some reason, it had never crossed my mind about Jessica packing a suitcase for the baby, and I was taken aback to see it. Neatly folded in the suitcase was diapers, adorable pink outfits, baby toiletries, hats, a condensed version of everything from her baby shower, and did she ever receive beautiful gifts! Jessica also packed some of the homemade blankets and quilts made by her auntie and friends. Just beautiful. Yes, we were really going to California to have this baby, and the suitcase proved it was true.

The couple of days leading up to our flight were a blur to me, and I can't recall much of what went on. I can't help but believe that God was protecting me from the impact of leaving as things were moving along smoothly and we were right on target with all that we needed to get done.

October 19: The Day
We Leave for California

The big day had finally arrived. After the unexpected news that Jessica was pregnant, to the shocking revelation about the baby having a heart condition, to the numerous medical appointments and tests, the insurance nightmare and hundreds of telephone calls going back and forth between medical facilities in Hawaii and California. The preparation of leaving my husband and family, my position at our company, and putting extra help into place, the baby shower and shipping my car to California, it was time to physically leave our Aloha State and set off on this mission. I woke up that morning feeling anxious yet with a spirit of surrender. There was no going back now. This was as real as it gets, and it was time for me to put on my armor to protect my daughter and to usher her brand new baby girl into this world.

CJ's parents came to our house to help transport our entire luggage to the airport and to see their son off. CJ had never been away from his parents for any length of time and so this was especially hard for him. While the suitcases were being loaded into our vehicles I stood out on the front stairs of my home for a minute. I watched our bags disappear into the trunks of our cars and I suddenly felt weakened with nervousness. I know one day when my daughter reads these words she's going to wonder what exactly was I so afraid of. Change has never been one of my greatest assets. My life, though full as it was, was very routine – work, swim, church, family, dinners with friends. We didn't travel much, and I was not much of an adventurer since my children were born. This was stepping way out of my box. It was not easy being responsible for not only Jessica and CJ but also apprehensive of what was ahead of us with Athena's birth.

I kissed my dog's goodbye and wondered if I'd see Zoë again. She had even come to work with me since she was a puppy and we were inseparable. As I was leaving, I whispered in her ear, even though she couldn't hear well, to hold on for me until I got home, and then closed the glass sliding door behind me. I kissed my finger and held it against the glass as she watched me leave. Goodbye, my precious Zoë.

In the middle of our cul-de-sac, CJ's parents, CJ, Jessica, my husband and I discussed our plans once we arrived at the airport, then off we went in our cars. I took a long last look at our home, wondering when we'd be back again, and looked the other way.

"When we come back, we will return with a baby," I told myself, trying to focus on why we were doing this and to stop myself from crying. My dearly loved home of 30 years, the same home that I carried my own first newborn over the threshold of – where the same hallways were now to echo with the sounds of my daughter's daughter. It was such an unbelievable thought thinking we'd return home with this baby that we've watched grow through 3D ultrasound photos and listen to her heartbeat time and time again. The baby that would be facing grueling open – heart surgery right after she was born. Our Athena Marie.

At the airport, CJ cried when kissing his parents goodbye. Jessica hugged her dad and I held onto him like a child afraid to leave their parent on the first day of school. We kissed and I walked away, a few steps behind CJ and Jessica who walked hand in hand. I'm all by myself now. I had never faced a mission of such magnitude – so far from home. But here I was. Flying to a state that I would soon be driving in...living in. Unfamiliar with every aspect of our lives ahead of us. The great unknown.

My sister Gloria, who lived in California, was originally going to stay with us at a condo that my mom owned in a neighboring city, about an hour and a half away from the hospital where Jessica would deliver Athena and where she would have her surgery. No one was living in the condo at the time, and we would be staying there until Jessica's due date grew closer and room became available for us at the Ronald McDonald House.

Gloria knew her way around this area as her own daughter had once been hospitalized at Stanford years ago. She would help us navigate to the hospital and back to moms until we could do it on our own.

Months before, we had contacted the Ronald McDonald House in Palo Alto, California, and filled out the necessary paperwork to be able to stay there. It was never guaranteed that space would be available when you needed it. But with the right criteria, you were welcomed to stay. This particular Ronald McDonald House would allow four people to a room, which would include Athena after she was born. It was a facility only for sick children and their families, and what a beautiful place it turned out to be. It was just minutes away from Stanford and had shuttle busses running to and from the hospital every half an hour. We were hoping to be there at least a week before Jessica gave birth so that we would be close to the hospital when she went into labor. That is, if there was room for us.

Just two weeks before we were to leave for California, Gloria got her results from her annual mammogram, and had to have a breast biopsy. I was in a complete state of disbelief when she called me to say that the tumor they had detected on the X-ray was malignant – she had breast cancer! Thank God, they found it early, at stage two. She therefore could not make the trip to stay with us as her treatment of a lumpectomy; chemotherapy and radiation were to start soon. I was stunned that my sister had cancer and was sick with worry about her. She was my best friend, and I was looking so forward to her being there with us. She has always been a great source of comfort to me and having to now do this without her felt like another slap in the face. What else, God? Why her? Why now? Why?

Gloria felt terrible that she couldn't be at the airport to welcome us with the hugs and kisses we looked forward to. There's nothing like flying across the ocean and having your family there once getting off the plane. But in light of everything else, this was the least of our problems. She and my mother arranged to have a limousine pick us up from the Sacramento Airport and drive us to her condo. Mom didn't drive, and Gloria was in no condition to be driving long distances especially after learning the news.

After we arrived at the Honolulu airport, we checked in at the counter and were assigned our seats in row 11. The number 11 had become of special interest to us, as Jessica was born on August 11 and CJ on May 11. Jessica proclaimed months ago that Athena would be born on November 11, even though her due date wasn't until November 27. Now, we were to sit in row 11 on the plane. At this point, I started thinking that I wouldn't be one bit surprised if Athena was indeed born on the November 11, just as Jessica said she would be.

Once we were finished checking in, and with boarding passes in hand, I asked for a wheelchair for Jessica, which they promptly provided. She had been on complete bed rest to prevent contractions and walking around the airport terminal was out of the question. Jess was embarrassed and initially refused to sit in one, but there was no negotiating with me so down she sat.

After we passed through the security line, we found a restaurant where we sat down to kill some time as we still had an hour and a half before our plane boarded. Each one of us was dealing with this time in our own separate way and we made small talk while sitting there. CJ talked about how he never really left home before and I knew this was a big challenge for him. As much as he liked to think of himself as a "grown up," he was still very much attached to his family, and I adored him for that.

Even though he and Jessica had broken up he was going to be there for the birth of his daughter and to be of support to Jessica. It was an unusual situation but not uncomfortable for me. I had known CJ since he was a boy and cared about him in light of what was going on between him and Jess. I wasn't always happy about the things he did but he was only 20 years old, and his behavior was pretty much par for the course, and I never held it against him.

Once boarding the plane, we quickly found our seats, and they couldn't have been more perfect. Three middle seats for the three of us. We were in the bulkhead, in the middle section of the plane, with no one sitting in front of us. There was a large screen right on the wall to watch the movie on. Right after taking off, CJ took some Benadryl and quickly went to sleep. Jessica told me that he didn't like to fly and every time he and his family flew they would take Benadryl and sleep through the flight. Jessica wasn't happy about him going to sleep, but she knew ahead of time that this was the way he dealt with flying so she was prepared. Jessica closed her eyes from time to time, and when she heard the food cart stopping by our seats she ordered two meals, one for her and one for CJ to have when he woke up. I can't recall what I ate, but I remember having a beer. After my drink, I zoned out for a short while before Jessica told me that she was having contractions.

Dear God, can anything else possibly scare the living daylights out of me? I swear, my adrenal glands were working overtime, and I worried that I might eventually just drop from the fright of it all. I reminded myself that she was on medication to slow down the contractions and played out all the different scenarios in my head of what could happen. Even if she was in labor, I think she would have labored more than three hours. The pilot could radio the hospital and let them know, and there'd be an ambulance waiting for us at the airport, or even a helicopter if need be. One thing that I learned during this journey of ours was that I have a wild and unrestrained imagination.

Some of the flight attendants noticed that Jessica was pregnant and sweetly asked her about her pregnancy. She always smiled and never said a word about anything being wrong. During one of Jessica's trips to the bathroom, I told one of the attendants a short, condensed version of our story, how we were flying to California for her to deliver her baby and how Athena would need heart surgery once she was born. Jess never ever wanted me to talk about this to anyone, but I found it so unbelievable that I wanted everyone to know. People's reaction was always the same – total amazement. This was such a rare thing to happen, and I never once met anyone who had ever heard of anything like this before. Jessica was experiencing a situation that most people, in their lifetimes, will never know. I wanted to share what she was going through because in my eyes, she was my hero.

When the wheels of the plane touched down in California, I could actually feel my body let down from all of the tension inside while in the air. For so long, I had been worried about Athena being born in Hawaii with no doctors to intervene. And with Jessica having contractions prior to our departure and while on the plane, I felt on edge all of the time. I later learned, and I don't know for the life of me why no one ever told us this before, that there could have been some type of medical intervention that would have sustained her until she was medivaced to California, had she been born in Hawaii. Nevertheless, I thanked God that we were finally in California – the safe side of the ocean. If my back wasn't so sore from sitting, I probably would have knelt down and kissed the ground.

Here we were now exiting the plane. It felt so good walking into the terminal and feel the cool crisp air of Sacramento. October is still so warm in Hawaii and the humidity is high. I felt energized walking out into this drastic, fresh change of temperature. The cold air gave us a boost of energy that we all needed. It was late, and we were beat.

The weeks and months leading up to this unparalleled journey of ours was now really happening. This is it! It was real! We were here! The people at our airport in Hawaii look much different from the people here. People dressed warmer, not the Aloha shirts and shorts that we are used to seeing people dressed in twelve months out of the year. We may as well have landed in another country, as the look and feel of everything was already so incredibly different.

Gratefully, we did not have to wait long for our bags. I stood there in the midst of the crowd waiting for their luggage, and I wondered about the story of their lives. Why were they landing in Sacramento? Was there anyone else on the plane that had a pregnant daughter who needed to give birth to a baby that needed heart surgery? I was never looking for sympathy from anyone, and looking back on it, I can't fully describe what I was feeling. I think it was just all too much to for me to keep inside. I just wanted people to know so that they could be thankful for their lives and that they were not in our shoes. No one should have been in this position, especially my daughter.

After we retrieved our bags we walked out to the front of the airport where limos and busses only were allowed to wait for their passengers. Here, we met our driver, whose name I can't recall, but what a sweet man he was. I believe he was one of the many people we would meet who was meant to be there, at that very date in time. I believe that God had appointed him to be the first one to greet us after we landed. He was a sweet spirited gentleman who welcomed us more like family members than customers. I just remember feeling so incredibly safe, so extremely relieved, that we were on the right side of the ocean and close to the hospital.

Athena was safe now.

Jessica and CJ, naturally, were excited with the limo: black and sleek looking with rope lights all around the black leather interior; all the ringers and bells, lights and TV screens, champagne decanters and long stemmed crystal glasses. While they nestled close to one another taking pictures, all I thought about was how good it felt to stretch out my sore back and finally be able to let my guard down. The ride took about an hour, and I felt like a child taking a road trip in our family car with my dad driving. I sat there with my head leaned against the cold window relaxing to the hum of the vehicle and bumps in the road. During that ride, I looked out of the tinted windows into this dark, vast and unfamiliar territory. I thought about how I'd soon be driving on these roads including the very highway we were traveling on. I just couldn't imagine driving and not having a clue of where I was.

The limo driver pulled up to the gated entrance of The Lighthouse Condominiums and pressed the intercom pad to ring my mom's unit. She was not living there at the time but came down from her Northern California home to get it ready for us. She remotely opened the wide black iron gate, and the driver drove through the complex, searching for mom's unit. In the dark, my mom appeared out of nowhere with a smile that could have lit up the night and she guided the driver towards the entrance of her beautiful town home.

I left home, at 18, and at 58, I had been away from California for 40 years. I had remained in close contact with my mom, calling her almost every day, visiting her once or twice a year when my kids were younger and remembered her on each holiday. I was extremely close to her in light of living so far away. Once I saw her, my inner child manifested and I felt so much love for this person whose heart I will have ever been closest too, while in her womb – my mother.

Jessica and CJ were delighted with Mom's condo and loved the intimate set up. It was a two-bedroom unit with each bedroom on opposite sides of each other with the open living and dining room area separating the two quarters. Jessica was immediately thrilled that their bedroom had its own bathroom and a walk-in closet, something we didn't have back home. Mom's living room had a small balcony right outside of the living room that CJ would eventually make his own. This was where, on the days that followed, he spent his quiet time smoking cigarettes and drinking a beer – his little dwelling place when he needed to be alone. I'd often see him outside with his yellow paper tablet on the table, writing lyrics to the songs he was composing. It was sweet to see him out there, in the cool of the evenings, and I often wondered what thoughts were going through his head.

Mom had forewarned me before we arrived that she had the large wall in the living/dining room painted orange, and I was dreading the thought of seeing it. I normally felt uncomfortable around bold colors but to my surprise, it was warm and beautiful. Just being there was beautiful. I can't quite explain it, but all the months of worry were now replaced with warmth, love, safety, relaxation and most of all, HOPE.

Jessica, CJ, Mom and I all sat in the living room talking and laughing well into the early morning hours. Three of us celebrated with a drink, while Jessica stuck to her fruit juice.

Over the years when I'd visit mom back home, she would always tell me to sleep in the bed with her, which I would always decline. But this year was different. That night, after we were all talked out and tired beyond measure, I crawled into bed with mom and her beloved 14-year-old poodle Toto (By the way, mom's name is Dorothy!), and we didn't sleep for a couple of more hours. I knew that I had another long day ahead of me when I got up, but I was filled with so much adrenaline from all that we had just been through. I relished this time of talking and giggling with my mom into the wee hours of the morning. Jessica had her mommy with her and I now had mine with me.

The plan for the following day was that my brother, who also lived in the same town as Mom, would come to the condo, and drive the kids and me to Matson, where I would pick up my car. I thought about my car, how it has sailed across the ocean, and I felt excited at the thought of being reunited with it. After we picked it up, Steve would guide us to Stanford, where Jessica was scheduled for a battery of tests and appointments that would keep us there well into the late afternoon. Then, after she was done, I would follow Steve as he guided us back to mom's condo in Vallejo.

When I woke up that morning, I was in a daze and couldn't figure out where I was at first. It took me a few moments for my brain to reboot and realize I was at moms. I looked at the clock and quickly jumped out of bed to check on Jessica.

Even with now being in California I still hovered over her like a mother hen. I quietly pushed open the door to their room and could hear her lightly snoring even before I saw her. She looked peaceful – her long hair draped over her shoulder and her body contoured around her pregnancy pillow. Jessica had started snoring in the latter part of her pregnancy, which I though was cute. But she was embarrassed and worried that she would keep CJ awake at night by it. That was my daughter, always worrying about CJ's comfort before her own.

I splashed some cold water on my face and put on the coffee. One thing I especially loved about visiting mom is that she would always make my coffee in the morning. Back home, I was the coffee maker while Ron made the bed. It was always a treat for mom to make me that first cup of the day when I visited her. But that day was different. With tremendous gratitude of her being there for me during this vulnerable time of my life, it was time for me to mother my mother, to make her a cup and serve it to her in bed.

I barely got four hours of sleep and felt exhausted. I worried about how I would be able to make it through the long day ahead of us with the fatigue I felt. The months leading up to this very day were behind me now, but I was drained from the stress I'd been under for so many months.

A little before 10 a.m., my brother Steve arrived at mom's ready to take us to the Matson Navigation Company in Oakland where my car was waiting for me. It felt wonderful seeing my big brother again, as it had been awhile since we'd last been together. As soon as he walked in the door, we embraced, and I buried my face into his chest and held onto him for a while. He was my protector and closest buddy when we were young and growing up in San Francisco. Although we had lived an ocean apart for so many years, the bond we shared was never broken. Big brother was here now and all was well. After a quick cup of coffee, off we went on our first big adventure in the golden state of California.

I thought it was utterly amazing that my sweet sedan had

sailed across the Pacific Ocean to be part of this journey with us, and I couldn't wait to see her.

Some people didn't understand why I shipped my car to California instead of renting one. As I explained so many times before, when your life has been turned upside down, when everything in front of you in unfamiliar, and when you are completely out of your comfort zone, something as simple as having your own car with you makes all of the difference in the world. I later realized what a truly wise decision of bringing it there was. There would be days that followed when I felt extremely anxious when driving on the freeways and to ease my anxiety, I would often imagine that I was driving back home and being in my own car helped to calm my jangled nerves.

The plan for the day was that after Steve drove us to pick up my car he would guide Jessica, CJ and me to Stanford and remain there with us until it was time to return to Vallejo. Jessica had several appointments that day, and I knew I wouldn't be able to find my way back to moms by myself. My car had a navigation system, but we didn't have time to program it yet, so Steve was my lifeline. I had been visualizing driving on these freeways for months and now the time had come – the day was here – where I'd be putting those imaginary driving skills to use. Athena was really going to be born, and for the very first time, we were going to the medical center of where all of this would take place. As independent as I thought I was, I realized how very much I depended on my husband. But he was taking care of our business and the home front while I was taking care of our daughter. We have always worked together as a team since our children were little, and now it was time for me to go solo.

Since Jessica became pregnant my life had been spread so thin, balancing all of the things that most women do and then some. Besides running our own company, which required tremendous focus, I meticulously ran our household, swam several miles a week and was very involved in our church ministry. Overseeing Jessica's care was my top priority, and I would drop whatever I was doing on the dates of her doctor's appointments or whenever she needed help with anything.

The day we left for California, most of that was put aside, even though I would remotely log into my computer at work to do what I needed to do. My sole purpose now was to safeguard my daughter throughout the remainder of her pregnancy and to bring Athena into this world at the accredited hospital that was waiting for her. Whatever came my way, I knew I would be able to handle it.

The drive to Oakland to pick up my car was nerve-wracking. My brother drove a standard BMW 325 sedan. My Infinity M45 was a smooth riding, quiet, comfortable full-sized vehicle, while his car was more like a sports car, which fit his personality perfectly. Steve, a well-seasoned driver on the California freeways, drove faster that I would have and changed lanes far more often that I would. But this was the same brother than I rode on the back of his motorcycle when we were teenagers, and I trusted him completely. He wasn't doing anything wrong, I was just hyper vigilant about everything. I was so nervous about Jessica's well-being – even though Athena was safe and sound – I still constantly worried about her. I was anxious for her birth and couldn't wait to meet her – but in the same token, I knew once she entered this world, and knowing what she would have to face, I somehow wished that she could have stayed where she was forever. I'm sure she probably enjoyed the bumpy car ride but I didn't. I just wanted this day to be over with.

The Matson port in Hawaii somehow seemed bigger than the one in Oakland. The process of dropping off my car was a lot more complex that picking it up. Steve parked his car and we all entered a small office where all I had to do was show my identification, sign some paperwork, and I was soon handed the key to my vehicle. When I first saw my car, I was so excited. My sister and I had come to the conclusion, that since we have both been through such life-changing events, we have become supersensitive about everything. Even seeing my car for the first time in weeks brought tears to my eyes.

I looked at my car and thought about how she was going to be part of this journey, getting us to and from where we needed to be, and how eventually, Athena would be riding in her backseat. It felt amazing to sit down in the driver's seat and to drive away to where I didn't quite know, but my brother would lead us there.

Once leaving Matson, with CJ and Jessica on board, we followed Steve as we traveled to Stanford University Hospital in Palo Alto. I may as well have been in a foreign country as everything was unfamiliar. The skies were gray, a huge contrast to our clear blue Hawaiian skies back home. I was tense as I drove, as the freeways were a hundred times busier than our freeways in Honolulu.

Palo Alto is a beautiful city that I would eventually come to love. Stanford was a vast medical facility, and we initially had a difficult time finding the office of where we first needed to be. I thought that everyone who Jessica met would be impressed that she was from Hawaii and how she traveled so far to be at this facility. But I soon learned that people came to this medical center from all over the country and being from Hawaii was apparently no big deal to anyone we came in contact with.

We first met with her appointed obstetrician across the street from the main hospital. I will never forget this day, entering this office for the first time. The reception area was filled with sunlight streaming through huge windows behind the long counter. Jessica looked so beautiful with her trademark plumeria flower pinned behind her ear with her waist long wavy Hawaiian hair draping over her shoulder. She turned heads everywhere she went. As I caught people's eyes on her, I thought to myself as I did time and time again, "If they only knew." If they only knew that in light of her beautiful outer layers, her spirit was filled with angst. Her pregnancy looked beautiful to others but deep inside of her soul she was filled with apprehension and fear.

My brother Steve had a chronic back condition, and I was concerned with him having to wait most of the day with us.

We really didn't know how long we'd be there, but he was in it for the long haul.

As Jessica met with the very first doctor, Steve stretched out on a padded bench outside the obstetrician's office in the hallway. I went out there a couple of times to let him know what was going on and how much longer I thought it would be until she was done. I felt so bad seeing him lying down as I knew he was in pain. But that was my big brother. Loving me enough to be there for me, no matter how bad he felt.

Once we were finished with that appointment we got into our cars and drove across the street to the hospital side of this magnificent and renowned medical center for our next appointment.

As we walked around the grounds of this huge hospital, we must have looked like a group of lost children. Thank goodness for the great security staff on the premises, as we had to stop and ask for directions a couple of times. I felt like Dorothy as she traveled the yellow brick road with her entourage to find the wonderful Wizard of Oz.

The next test Jessica was scheduled for was the infamous NST (Neonatal Stress Test), which she had so many times before. Jessica was led into another beautiful room, with laminate floors and uncovered windows that showcased the meticulous hospital grounds. The doctor's offices that Jessica was seen at in Hawaii couldn't hold a torch to the beauty of this place. You could feel the brilliance of this teaching hospital in the air. Everywhere you turned, not only were there doctors and nurses but students and interns. It was simply fascinating.

Jessica lay down, and the straps were adjusted around her big belly to monitor Athena's heartbeat. Once finished, the next test that followed was an ultrasound. There appeared to be fluid in the baby's stomach and she was told that if it was still there during her follow up visit, they would probably induce her labor. Jessica lamented, as she did time and time again, "Nothing ever seems to go right." She said this so many times during her pregnancy and every time I heard her say it, I felt all the more sad. This was supposed to be a wonderful time of her life, but from the very get go something was always hanging on the hinges.

We were at the hospital and clinic for over six hours and it was starting to get dark. I continued to worry about my brother's back, and I was feeling anxious about the drive home. I would follow Steve as he guided us back to Mom's and the thought of driving in the dark was nerve-racking.

By the time we got on the road, I was beyond exhausted. It was a feeling of fatigue that I hadn't felt before and it concerned me. We had only landed the night before and the combination of jet lag, worry, lack of sleep and nervousness about driving all seemed to hit me just as we got on the road. I remember about half way through the drive I felt like I couldn't go on. My mind felt weary and I knew at that moment that I just had to buckle down and bear it. I never wanted the kids to worry. I never ever wanted to them to know when I felt afraid, when I was nervous or when I was tired. This was not the time to show my vulnerability. Jessica felt safe now that she was in California, and I didn't want to rob her of that feeling for a moment.

Just as we were nearing the exit on the freeway to the city where my mom lives, my brother radically changed about three lanes over to the exit that he just about missed. I was able to stay with him but my heart pounded from the unexpected maneuver. Following someone when you don't know where you are, in the dark and when you are exhausted beyond measure is an extremely difficult thing to do. But we did it and we were finally off the freeway. Thank God! It was just a matter of a few more minutes before we were at the gated entrance of mom's condo – and I couldn't wait.

When we walked through the front door of moms, I felt a sense of relief that I swear was close to that of giving birth. As I walked into the living room and saw my mom, I just wanted to sob. But, as I've learned to do so many times during my life, especially now, I put on a face of composure and you'd never be able to tell by looking at me, how terrible I felt.

Jess was scheduled to for her next appointment in exactly one week, and I knew that no matter what happened now, the baby would be safe. I thought about the many months back home – especially as the time grew closer to our trip, how I worried about Jessica going into labor and us not being in California. That worry was with me all of the time and I always felt on edge. It felt good to finally be able to put this very troublesome fear to rest.

I carried around the hard cover pink journal that I had started writing in before we left, thinking I would write about our experiences while in California. I started logging down Jessica's appointments, the locations of places we needed to drive to such as grocery stores and my brother's house. In big and bold letters, I wrote down my mom's address in the front of my book. I wanted to make sure that if I ever needed to call 911, just in case I panicked and lost my mind, I would have her address right in front of me.

We were excited about the week ahead of us, and we felt like we were given a permission slip to finally enjoy ourselves. We were still feeling the effects of jet lag and were on Hawaiian time, which was three hours earlier than California. We were worn out, and the thought of not having to go to a doctor's appointment or fly across an ocean felt great to all three of us. The first thing we did the next day, was sit in my car in the parking lot of mom's condo and program the GPS. For now, mom was with us, and she would be able to guide us around town to the local shopping areas. Mom didn't drive, and she didn't have the greatest sense of direction, but it sufficed just enough to make due.

After programming the GPS, we drove to the grocery store around noon to stock up the pantry and fridge. Rice was a staple in Hawaii and that was the first item on our list of things to buy as Jessica ate rice with almost all of her meals. I wanted to do all that I could to make sure CJ and Jessica were as comfortable as possible and having their favorite foods on hand was important. In the same shopping center, we immediately noticed a restaurant called L&L Barbeque –

a chain restaurant that originated in Hawaii! The kids could hardly believe their eyes when they saw it there! CJ and I both loved to eat raw fish, and before we left for California we wondered how we were going to get by without one of the foods we loved most. Well, our worries were over as L&L sold raw fish, too! Jessica was in seventh heaven as well as their menu carried some of her favorites back home. I once worried about her lack of weight gain but I didn't have to worry any longer. Her appetite was very much par for the course of a very pregnant mother to be.

We were utterly amazed while walking through the very first grocery store we went into, with the abundance of food and produce. Hawaii is paradise in many ways, with beautiful oceans and mountains, but what we lack is a variety of everything from food to furniture due to everything having to be shipped there. It was close to Halloween, and the kids were amused by the assortment of pumpkins for sale. We bought a couple of little ones and later that evening, they had fun scooping them out and carving faces. After they finished with the first one, we put a candle inside it and placed it on the wall of the darkened balcony and stood there admiring their masterpiece. Jessica, who had never spent much time in the kitchen, baked CJ's favorite sugar cookies that night, which we all enjoyed eating. It was wonderful to be feeling rather normal again – replacing worry with joy. Seeing Jess smiling and having fun rejuvenated me. Up until that point, most everything surrounding our lives was doctor's appointments, packing and paperwork. This night felt warm, relaxed and magical.

We stayed fairly close to home for the first few days but eventually ventured out to the Golden Gate Bridge lookout. Jessica was starting to get a little stir crazy and wanted to see the bridge. I was still uncomfortable with driving but wanted to see her happy, so off we went freeway and all. Even with her in the backseat, I thought about the precious cargo she carried within her and never exceeded the speed limit. Matter of fact, Jessica was always telling me that I drove too slowly. But I was always on the side of caution.

God forbid anything should happen – especially a car accident.

The bridge was as magnificent as always and she and CJ took their tourist pictures with the Golden Gate behind them. They constantly texted pictures to family and friends to keep them in the loop of what they were doing. What a great electronic era they lived in. To be able to keep the ones they loved close, in light of the distance that separated them, was simply the best.

On the way home from the bridge, we stopped at an authentic Pumpkin Patch farm, another thing you didn't see in Hawaii. I must say, if there was anything positive about being in California, it was the time of the year we were there. All of the trees changing color and the cool chilly air were a welcomed change of scenery for us. Pumpkins were everywhere, in all of the stores, and now at the farm. Jess and CJ had a blast picking out their pumpkins and taking pictures of each other. It was a good day.

The week quickly passed, and our upcoming trip to Stanford was now to be done solo –without my brother's help. Even if he could have come, it was time for me to pull my bootstraps up and do this on my own. Jessica's appointments were spread out over a two -day period and so I decided to rent a hotel room for the first night we were there. The Ronald McDonald House did not have room for us yet, but they were able to provide us with a list of hotels that offered discounts to Stanford's medical patients. The Ronald McDonald House was only a few minutes away from the hospital, and I continued to pray that space would open up for us as soon as possible.

On our way to Palo Alto, I discovered something that I had no way of knowing beforehand, but then again, how could I? I was afraid of driving over bridges! We had to cross the Oakland Bay Bridge to get there and seeing it from a distance as we were approaching it made my heart pound and my hands sweat. I remembered seeing photos of the 1989 San Francisco earthquake and how a portion of the top of the bridge had collapsed. I swear I learned what the term "white knuckles" meant that day as there was not a drop of blood in my hands when we got to the end of it. If ever there was a moment that I wanted out of, this was definitely one of them.

CJ always sat in the front seat and Jessica the back. I called CJ my navigator because even though the GPS directed us where to go, I relied upon him to confirm that I was on the right path. In California, the freeways go straight, left and right, with so many overhead signs displaying names and numbers of freeways. CJ and I really bonded during this time as I depended on him much more than he was aware of.

On this second trip to Stanford, we met with the doctor, who was going to be performing this most specialized and intricate heart surgery on Athena. CJ was impressed by Dr. Hanley's laid back manner and he reminded him of the TV show character House. The doctor thoroughly explained the surgery, drawing several diagrams and gave us a boost of confidence like no one had before. He stated that the success rate of the surgery was about 99 percent and when we left his office, we were the happiest we'd been yet. Everything in our world was right now. We felt a new surge of hope and continued on with Jessica's next appointment.

After the last appointment late in the afternoon, with our GPS leading us, we found our way to the hotel, which was about five miles away from the hospital. Upon opening the door, Jessica was mortified by the way it looked. The room was dingy looking with old fashion tapestry bedspreads, curtains and worn carpets. The microwave and mini refrigerator were dated. It was a dramatic contrast to the contemporary condo we were staying in. It by all means wasn't the Hilton, but it was neat and clean and the price was right. This entire trip, in the end, cost thousands of dollars, and so saving money where I could was important. Jessica was adamant about not staying there, and I frantically looked through the yellow pages of the phone book for other places to stay but couldn't find a room for under 200 dollars. I wasn't thrilled with the room either, but all that we had to do was sleep there, and it was almost evening anyhow. There were times when I felt impatient with Jessica, but it didn't last long. I couldn't imagine what it felt like to be in her position, going through what she was going through. I tried my best to keep her as comfortable as possible. But this is what we had to do and where we had to stay, just until the morning. She finally calmed down, and we ended up unpacking our things and prepared to spend the night.

Many years ago, I had watched the movie "Castaway" with Tom Hanks, which touched me in an uncanny way. I am not much of a movie person, but I watched that show over and over again. There was something so daunting about the storyline, and I never really did quite figure out why it moved me like it did. I eventually tucked the DVD away in the closet somewhere, but I never really forgot about it.

My sister and I, who are the closest of siblings, would often sign our names off to each other in cards and emails as "Wilson" and "Chuck." In the movie, Chuck was an employee of FedEx when the cargo plane he was flying on crashed in the middle of the ocean. After drifting overnight on a life raft, he ended up on a vacant, deserted island, with no food or water. Some of the packages on the submerged plane eventually washed to shore of the island he was on, and he opened them, looking for items to sustain himself. One of the packages contained a Wilson volleyball, which he tossed aside as it was of no use to him.

Well, as the story goes, one day, after cutting his hand and feeling complete hopelessness of no one finding him, he picked up the ball and threw it out of anger. He left blood from his hand on the ball and seeing that it almost looked like a face, he smudged it around to make it look like one. He flippantly named the volleyball Wilson and started talking to it out of utter desperation of being alone.

That ball was his only source of companionship for the five years he was stranded there. When Chuck made his final attempt to flee the island on a makeshift raft, he brought his beloved Wilson with him. And so as the story goes, he falls asleep and while drifting in the water, Wilson somehow gets loose. Once waking up and realizing Wilson is gone, he panics when he sees him in the distance bobbing away. After a futile attempt of trying to rescue him, and unable to do so because of the strong current, Wilson fades away into the vast ocean, eventually leaving his sight. The music that played during that scene was melodic and mournful. No matter how many times I watched that part of the movie, I always cried. Something so poignant about losing someone or something that you so desperately loved and needed.

My sister had found a replica of the same ball in a store and had my mother bring it to the condo in Vallejo. When we arrived there that first night, Wilson was sitting on my bed, waiting for me, and I sighed when I saw it. My sister was my Wilson, and I, her Chuck. Though we lived thousands of miles apart, the love we shared was immeasurable.

As it went, my sister couldn't be with me as we originally planned, and so Wilson stood proxy for her, going everywhere we did. I started taking pictures of him on our various outings, with the very first one of him sitting on my lap as I sat on a bench looking out to the Golden Gate Bridge. It was humorous to open my car door and see Wilson there in the back seat. After we unpacked our suitcases at the motel, I placed Wilson on the bed with me and every time I looked at that ball, I was reminded of my sister's love, and felt comforted by it.

The next day after we were finished with our appointments at Stanford, we stopped by the Ronald McDonald House to see exactly where it was located and to take a short tour. Jessica was not only adamant about staying at the hotel the night before; she did not want to stay at the Ronald McDonald House either. She was so vulnerable during this time and I knew she was fearful of seeing other sick children. She wasn't able to express how she felt with her words but her actions spoke loud and clear. I had to coach her like crazy just to get her in there and to explore the facility.

I was amazed at what I initially saw as we approached the beautiful building that looked like a five-star hotel with a grand entrance. Once you walked inside the door, you could immediately feel the home away from home environment.

We were shown the type of room that we would be staying in when a space, hopefully, became available. There was a double and single bed with modern, contemporary maple wood frames. Next to a big window that overlooked the beautiful streets of Palo Alto were a desk, chair, house phone, and a list of numbers to numerous departments of the facility. A caretaker also lived on the premises and could be reached 24 hours a day. The bathroom was big and bright with a large frosted privacy window that streamed natural daylight through. Everything was so modern and clean. There was a huge closet with built-in shelves that would provide enough storage space for all three of us and then some. There were only a few minor stipulations of the house that were strictly prohibited. Drugs and alcohols were absolutely forbidden, and there was no food allowed in the rooms. This made sense to me as keeping the house and rooms clean took precedence to keep it as germ-free as possible. There was no TV, but you could bring one in if you wanted to.

Over the next couple of weeks, I started getting nervous about whether or not a space would become available for us at Ronald McDonald House. I called once again on the morning of November 2, and was told that there was no room yet. Even though our name was placed on the list months ago, there was still no guarantee of a space becoming available when we needed it. Jessica' due date was growing near, and I wanted to be close to the hospital so I wouldn't have to drive an hour and a half to get there, God forbid, at night! I knew that if she went into labor I could make the drive, but I was certain that I would be a nervous wreck. I just wanted to be there already so that we could finally settle in and settle down before the big day arrived.

Back home, I regularly swam a mile about three or four days a week at our local district pool. I'd start work about 6 a.m., and stop at about 8 to swim. Then, it was back to work. Swimming was my passion, and it was not just beneficial for me physically but mentally as well. When I first pushed off the wall to begin my swim, I was able to leave the world behind for a little while. In the water I was in my element, and I absolutely thrived in it. Before I left Hawaii, I browsed the Internet searching for a pool close to moms, hoping that I'd be able to swim there once in a while. I found a pool a few miles away, so with everything else I packed for our two month stay, I packed all of my swim gear. Just thinking about packing now was something else. When you are going to be away for a weekend or a week, packing, especially as a woman, is hard enough. When you are planning to be away for two to three months, well, you end up bringing just about everything you own.

One day, while in Vallejo, I hesitantly decided that I would finally swim there and dug my gear out of my suitcase. I felt uncomfortable while getting ready, as I knew I would have to let my GPS guide me to the pool and I didn't know quite what to expect once I got there. It was November, and in the low 60's. I had no idea what the water temperature would be in this outdoor pool. Back home, we could swim outside all twelve months of the year. I'd put on my swimsuit and shorts and drive to the pool that was only five minutes away and swim with the regulars. Sometimes, in between laps, I'd stop in the shallow end of the pool to "talk story" with other swimmers who were also taking a moment to catch their breath.

I punched the address of the pool into my GPS, and off I went driving through the beautiful wide-open streets of Vallejo, adorned with fall leaves on the sidewalks. It was awkward driving to this pool where I had never been before in a total unfamiliar area. I was so out of my element that I may as well have been on Mars. I parked my car and looked at the pool through the fence watching the swimmers. I felt like the new girl on the first day of school, having to face a classroom in which I didn't know anyone. I was anxious when I walked into the facility and asked the attendant about the rules of their pool and the locker room. I'm sure everyone knew I wasn't from there, as most swimmers know each other. Even the direction they swam in was different. Back home, we were allowed to swim the entire length of the Olympic size 50-meter pool. At this pool, you had to swim the width of the pool. Instead of having to swim back and forth 15 times for a mile, I had to swim the width and back 30 times, which I didn't like at all. Too much unnecessary time on turns. But that was me, looking for the most efficient and quickest way of doing anything and everything, including swimming.

That was the first time I had swam in weeks and my stamina had diminished from the long absence of swimming. I fell asleep early that night and slept harder than I had in a while from the exercise. I was abruptly awakened at about 11:30 p.m., with Jessica standing next to my bed saying that she was having steady contractions. I felt disoriented when I shot up out of bed. We started timing her contractions and I silently pleaded with God to not let this happen this night. I was exhausted, and I worried about my ability to drive to the hospital feeling this way. Her contractions eventually stopped and I thanked God profusely for letting me off the hook. I knew right then and there, that I would not swim again. I had to save every bit of my energy to be prepared for whatever was before us and that was that. I packed away my swim gear and knew I wouldn't be seeing it again for a long time.

On November 8, I again called the Ronald McDonald House, and the woman I spoke with said that they just had an opening right before I called and to come right away. I asked if we could come the following day as we had so much to do to get ready plus the long drive to get there. She said if we didn't come today that she would have to give the room away to another family! I had been waiting for this moment for so long and couldn't believe that we were expected to come the minute an opening became available. I was beside myself and started to cry telling her how much we had been through and how hard this entire situation had been on all of us. She put me on hold for a short while then came back on the line saying that they would make an exception for us and hold our space until the following day. I hung up the phone weary of this emotional roller coaster that I simply wanted off from.

I was relieved that we were moving to the Ronald McDonald House yet sad to be leaving the condo. We were just starting to feel at home and comfortable with our new environment. Our main source of entertainment there during our stay was shopping. We especially liked looking at clothes and shopping at a discount store called "Dee Dees." Prices were so reasonable everywhere we went, and we liked the layered look of clothing – something we couldn't wear back home. I was at the point where I didn't have to use the GPS in Vallejo any longer and now here we were being uprooted once again.

Something about this condominium felt so safe to me. In Hawaii, our house certainly wasn't huge, but it was large in comparison to this space we were staying in. Our home is two stories while the condo was one. I loved the coziness of the condo and the close proximity of our quarters. Jess was in the bedroom on one side and I was in the other. In the middle of our rooms were the living, dining room and kitchen, which we all regularly congregated too. From the kitchen, while I cooked, I'd see CJ outside on the little patio area, in his own little zone, ear buds in, listening to music, smoking a cigarette and writing lyrics on his yellow tablet. I was pleased seeing him out there as he certainly needed an outlet. I knew he was having a hard time being away from his family and friends.

Our house in Hawaii has large open windows with no curtains as we were set up on a hill and you can't see into it from the street. It is bright year round with sunlight always illuminating the rooms. The condo only had windows on one side of the unit with not as much light, but it felt so soothing.

My mother left the condo the week before we did. Her

main home where she lives the majority of the year is in the same city as my sister's home in Grass Valley, California, which is about two hours away from Vallejo. She mainly stays at the condo when she visit's both of my brothers but came down about a week before our arrival to get it ready for us. Knowing that we would soon be moving to Palo Alto, she returned to Grass Valley to be with my sister who was beginning her cancer treatment. I really felt on my own now, just me and the kids heading into new territory.

Jessica was still so resistant about staying at the Ronald McDonald House and was irritable the entire drive there. I knew she was fearful of being around other families who struggled with their own children's health issues and I believe, was being confronted by her own feelings that she wouldn't express.

I have and will always believe in angels. The day that we checked in at the Ronald McDonald House, one was waiting for us.

When we walked through the front door, Joe, a volunteer of the house, gently greeted us. He was an older man, white wavy hair, in his mid to late sixties, soft-spoken, a little on the pudgy side. His voice was calming and his smile soothing. We all sat down on the couch of the beautiful foyer, near the front desk, while he went over the rules and regulations of the house and made our nametags and room keys. Jessica was having some mild contractions as we sat there. Joe placed his hand over his chest as if he was having heart palpitations. "You're not going to have the baby right now, are you?" he joked. He had a childlike playfulness about him, and his affectionate nature was just what Jessica needed at that moment – a grandfatherly figure welcoming us into this sanctuary in a loving, relaxed way.

After all of the paperwork was done, Joe walked us over to the elevator and took us up to our room. I had to contain myself once the door opened as we now were entering a safe haven. There was nothing that I had to be afraid of anymore. We were here! We were two minutes from the hospital, and all of the support that I needed was right at hand. No longer did I have to fear driving to the hospital in the middle of the night. Even during the day, the drive was hard on me. Just the thought of having my pregnant daughter in the car, on the freeway, alone, made me uneasy.

After we did our initial unpacking and we were more or less settled in our room, we walked around and checked out the entire facility in total amazement. I had never seen anything quite like this before. Jessica and CJ were also surprised by what they saw and I could see that Jessica was finally starting to relax.

The kitchen was huge with several islands of gas stoves and ovens. Each family was assigned its own small cupboards and a mini refrigerator to store their personal food items in. Everyone was also allowed use the large commercial fridge as well. The house provided all of the staples such as milk, bread, canned goods, Top Ramen, macaroni and cheese, peanut butter. I was told that every morning the kitchen counters were filled with hot and cold cereals, breads and gourmet pastries. There was an industrial-sized coffee maker, which made individual cups of coffee, along with regular coffee makers. There were vending machines with cold water and beverages, an ice machine, and a beautiful patio outside with gas grills and picnic benches. And if that wasn't enough volunteers would often bring in or cook dinners in the kitchen. And they weren't just any meals; they were wonderful fresh, nutritious homemade meals, with exception to Fridays. Every Friday, I was told, there was a list left out on the kitchen counter where you could write down what you wanted from McDonalds, one of the largest contributors to the Ronald McDonald House. At 5 p.m., without fail, all of the orders placed in individual bags would be delivered and waiting for the families on the kitchen counter. The dining room was large with floor to ceiling windows that showcased the beautiful fall scenery outside. The lush trees and perfect landscaping almost had a storybook feel to it. There was a statue of Ronald McDonald sitting on a bench in the patio which added to the fairy tale setting. There were laundry rooms with multiple washers and dryers on each floor with detergent provided at the front desk. There was a library, computer rooms, playrooms, and big screen TV rooms. Much to CJ's delight, there was also a gym there and he was thrilled! I don't think there was a hotel around that could compare to this. Due to the generosity of McDonalds and all of the contributors in the luxuriant city of Palo Alto, there was only a $10 a day charge per family. There was a shuttle bus that left every half-hour to the hospital, and that alone was the biggest bonus. The generosity of this facility and how it went above and beyond to make every family as comfortable as possible was astounding.

When I think about the term of God saying that he has provided many mansions for us in Heaven, I believed that He had just paved the way for one here for us on earth.

I never have been a big fan of change. My life was pretty much unadventurous back home in Hawaii, and I was very content in it. Everything about my day-to-day life was hectic but safe, consistent, routine. It's not that I didn't like adventure, but I was born with an above average responsible countenance – so responsible that I took it to the extreme. My husband often worked on the outer islands, and when my children were younger, I had ample opportunities to travel and work with him. But I did not like the thought of us being on the same plane together. I was never afraid of death; I simply was fearful of leaving my children without either of their parents. My own mother had lost her mom when she was only twelve, and I could see how it affected her life. So, Ron and I rarely traveled together. Our joy had always been watching and supporting our children in their sporting activities right in our own little home town. Like most all parents, our children were the treasures of our lives.

There I was, in a different state, in a brand new communal environment, not knowing a soul, preparing for my daughter to give birth to a child who would need heart surgery. My life felt like the pockets of my husband's pants before I washed them: turned upside down and inside out.

There was nothing about my present life now that vaguely resembled my life back home. Although I remotely logged into work, edited reports, and took care of the company finances, it was minor compared to the day-to-day operation of the business. I had managed this company for almost 30 years, and working was like breathing to me. Before we left for California, I spent a lot of time worrying about how I would adapt to not working full time, but unbeknownst to me I was adjusting to it just fine. At the Ronald McDonald House, I felt relieved that I would no longer have to be driving long distances, and that alone was a huge load lifted from me. After all this time of taking care of and protecting Jessica, and CJ, I now felt in safe hands and supported with something tangible to lean on.

I could spend the rest of my life thanking the Ronald McDonald House. I later learned there were so many people who wanted to volunteer there that they actually had to turn some away. Wednesday dinners eventually became my favorite, as it was soup night. A local organization brought in about five different types of homemade soups in large crock-pots with a variety of specialty breads. Soup, in my humble opinion, is certainly, as they say food for the soul. I had so many marvelous memories of the soups that my mom made during my childhood, and here I was, tasting that love once again.

I was always concerned about Jessica's nutrition, and I cooked as often as I could. Now, there were others contributing to her care, and I was so very grateful. I still cooked some of her favorites from time to time but I was able to start saving more energy for Athena's arrival. At this point, I was mentally worn down yet so still so physically strong.

There were two beds in our room. Jess and CJ slept in the double bed while I had the twin, separated from theirs by a nightstand. For some reason, I didn't feel uncomfortable sharing the same room with them even though I'm an extremely private person. We had been through so much together and it felt natural to be sharing the same space. I'd often refer to us as the "Three Musketeers" as we certainly were a team.

On every floor of the house, including the one that we were on, there was a spacious communal "living room" with couches, chairs and a big screen TV. On the first floor, was the kitchen with four cooking areas, each one with a full sized stove, a sink, dishwasher, pots and pans and cupboards with every kind of utensil and pot imaginable. It was actually four kitchens combined into one. Everyone had their favorite place to do their own cooking if they wanted to. There were several families who regularly cooked in the evenings, and it was fun seeing the different types of ethnic foods they prepared. I found my own little niche at the rounded end of one of the cooking islands that had electrical outlets for appliances. This became my spot where early in the morning and later in the afternoon I'd pull up a stool, plug in my laptop, and log into my office. I would occasionally Skype with my husband, and some of my friends from the house would stand behind me and wave to Ron. I especially loved it when he held my dogs on his lap so I could see them.

Unless you have experienced it firsthand, it is difficult to explain the dynamics of living in a communal home such as the Ronald McDonald House. Though all of us came from many different places, we had so much in common. We were all there for our children. There was a Latino woman who didn't speak a lick of English, and I not an utterance of Spanish. But every time we saw each other, we both smiled. She'd say, "Hola" while I said "Aloha." We'd often greet with a hug and in our own way, we'd ask each other how things were going. She'd use her hands to ask about my daughter by motioning her hand over her stomach, depicting the outline of a pregnant belly. I'd shake my head and say, "No, not yet." Her child was being treating for cancer, and in the best way she could, she was able to communicate to me that he was doing well.

The very first night we were there, I slipped into the TV room and turned on my favorite news channel, which I had not been able to receive at moms. I curled up on the sofa and nestled in like a kitten on a rug. It had been awhile since I was able to catch up on the politics that my husband and I so closely followed back home, and I was in heaven. I felt completely at peace with my mind free of worry. Jessica was safe, the hospital was two minutes away, and I was finally able to let go.

The next evening, I was in the same room, on the same sofa, watching another one of my favorite programs when Jessica walked in and told me she was having contractions. By this time, she had so many of them over the months that I didn't react the way I once did. And now that we were so close to the hospital, I had no reason to be afraid. I leisurely got up and walked down the hall to our room, and we started timing them. It wasn't long before I knew this was probably it and had CJ call the hospital to tell them we were on our way. The three of us grabbed our things with Jessica taking her well-prepared hospital bag. We took the elevator down to the parking lot, got in my car, and drove to the prominent Stanford Hospital.

As we walked into the lobby of this amazing medical center, I was overcome with emotion knowing that Athena, most likely, would be born on November 11, just as Jessica said she would. How I already loved this baby in the most instinctual way!

I felt sad knowing that these were the last hours that she would be at peace in her mother's womb before entering this world and undergoing such grueling surgery.

It was hard trying to maintain a strong front for my daughter and CJ right then, as I was extremely anxious of all that was before us. If there ever was a time that I wished my husband could have been with me, it was that moment.

Soon after we arrived at the hospital, Jess was examined, and it was confirmed – she was in labor and three centimeters dilated! So here we were. After all the weeks and months leading up to this point, after all of the doctor's appointments back in Hawaii, the preparation for this huge journey, the unbelievable paperwork involved...the emotions we had to contain...the three of us preparing to be away from our lives and setting sail to my car across the Pacific Ocean...flying 2500 miles to a whole new environment...getting comfortable at mom's...becoming familiar with the roads of this foreign state we were in, being uprooted once again, traveling to the Ronald McDonald House, and just the next day – after we arrived and just getting settled in – Athena was ready to enter our worlds. The time was here, the time was now, and I just couldn't have been more ready to meet her. All of the tension leading up to this moment was so built up inside of me I felt like a helium balloon, ready to burst.

After Jessica's examination was through, she and CJ walked around the halls of the hospital for a while before she was checked into the room that Athena would later be born in.

Jessica wanted to have Athena naturally and wrestled with the decision of whether to have an epidural or not. She knew that I had all three of my children naturally. But when she got to about five centimeters, she became increasingly uncomfortable and more anxious about making her decision. Not long after, one of the nurses told her that it would probably be best, for Athena's sake, to have the epidural. So with great apprehension, she agreed. The staff at the hospital was so kind and compassionate to Jessica and made this moment for her as relaxed as possible.

While she was being prepped for the procedure, I sat in front of her as she leaned forward with her legs over the edge of the hospital bed. It brought me back to the moment that she sat in my office, with her legs dangling over a desk telling me that she was pregnant. And now here I was, with this daughter of mine whom I had become joined by the hip to, as she prepared for the birth of her first child. Her baby girl, who would be taken away from her the moment she was born and whisked away by the Neonatal Intensive Care Team.

As she leaned forward and while the anesthesiologist poked the needle into her spine, I sat there, as usual, with my poker face. So many times I felt like screaming, "I don't want to be here, I don't want to do this." This was another one of those times. I didn't want to watch this. I had immense faith in the doctors and nurses there but I worried about that small percent of something going wrong. That was one thing I had become an expert at through this whole entire experience: worrying about the worst-case scenario of everything.

A staff member of Lucille Packard Children's Hospital, the children's side of Stanford, told us that they had developed their own epidural formula, warding off the pain yet still letting you feel in control of your lower body. Not long after Jessica had the injection she felt complete relief of the contractions, and with a smile on her face, soon fell fast asleep.

In this large labor and delivery room, there was a small little alcove with a built-in cushioned area to sleep on. CJ offered it to me, but I knew that I wouldn't be able to sleep. How could I? I could have run a marathon with all of the adrenalin racing through my body. So CJ lay down and he too fell asleep while I sat in a hard chair next to Jessica's bed watching the monitors. It was so strange to see her contractions happening on the screen while Jessica slept through them all, not feeling any one of them.

During the middle of the night, in the darkened room illuminated only by the machines that were tracking the course of her contractions and Athena's heart rate, I couldn't help but flash back to the time when my husband had a brain aneurysm and I kept vigil by his bedside in the critical care unit. I somehow allowed myself to slip back there for a few moments and remembered the fear of him dying. Our children were young at the time and we were running our company together in full throttle. No matter what alarm went off on any of those machines; I felt terrified and immediately pushed the nurse's button. Now, here I was, watching my daughter's contractions on the monitors while she slept so soundly, so safely. I watched the peaks and valleys of Jessica's contractions, as they grew closer of expelling Athena into our lives. The room was cold, much like my husband's hospital room, and it was eerie. I felt delirious during the early morning visits from the nurses who cracked opened the door of the room to check on Jessica and the monitors with a flashlight. But there I sat, in that uncomfortable chair, with the determination of a mother's love, watching over my daughter, waiting, worry, praying. I just couldn't believe that Jessica could sleep through her labor. The whole concept of being in labor with no pain was so foreign to me and seemed entirely against the grain of nature.

My first child, my son, was not only born naturally, but he was in a breech position when delivered. By the time the doctor realized he was breech, I was already in the throes of contractions. They immediately started preparing me for a C-section, but Matthew decided to come on his own terms and the doctor couldn't stop him. Now, all three of my children have Hawaiian middle names, and his is Hekili, meaning, "thunder." His birth certainly lived up to that name as he came in such a thunderous manner. He was my first baby, and so I didn't have anything to compare his birth to.

Morning came, and I was thankful for the daylight. In that dark and cold room, while Jessica labored and CJ slept, I felt alone and exhausted. The light of day gave me a sense of reassurance and the increased activity and sounds of the hospitals hustle and bustle comforted me. Once waking up, Jessica felt rested and CJ refreshed. I found my way to a coffee cart and bought the biggest cup of the darkest roast I could find. The true marathon was before us, and I needed something to give me a boost to make up for the sleep that I forfeited that night while keeping watch over my girl.

Around 10:30 a.m., everything started to change and the tone of the room took on a more serious note. There was a flurry of activity going on and I swear, I felt like I was watching the filming of a TV show. We were informed well ahead of time that there would be at least 10 other people in the room when Athena was born. The NIC team started setting up their area to prepare for their interception of her.

When I saw them roll in the little plastic cubicle type bassinet that babies are placed in after they are born it felt surreal to think that she would soon be lying inside of it. Within the tiny enclosure was a little package containing the first diaper they would later put on her, her wristband, and some other items. I walked over and took a picture of it for our scrapbook. I was tired from not sleeping and apprehensive of what was ahead but I was so ready for her birth.

It was well after noon and Jessica was fully dilated. CJ called his mom and me, my daughter, Kendra whom I missed terribly. We turned the speakers of our cell phones on so they could all hear the birth of Athena. Now, all that Jessica had to do was push and this long awaited miraculous miracle of ours would be here.

The room was packed with doctors, nurses, interns and students. Their faces were somber, like a crowd standing next to an air traffic controller who was attempting to help land a plane in trouble. It was awkward. I had to do something to lighten the moment, so I joked with the doctor saying, "At least in the old days, there was some screaming going on," to which he and the nurses laughed. All of us just stood there watching Jessica with her legs spread wide apart with her cell phone in hand, waiting for another contraction to push. I am thankful that my daughter was not modest like me and able to keep a light spirit during this time. I cannot count how many people commented on her positive attitude. I reveled in those last moments of Jessica being without child. For us mothers, we know that giving birth is the easy part. Once your child is born, a sense of responsibility like no other comes along with it, and your heart no longer belongs to yourself.

Athena is Born

And then I had the first glimpse of this baby for who we waited forever for, whose birthday would indeed be November 11, just as Jessica willed it to be. Every single second, from the time Jessica announced her pregnancy, up until this moment, flashed before me in fast forward. No matter how old or young you are, no matter what you have or have not been through in your life, there is nothing that compares to bearing witness to a child being expelled from its mother's womb. To see your daughter giving birth, giving life to her child – well, for a mother, it's a feeling beyond words.

The first thing I saw as she was crowning was a little crop of dark, almost black hair. I stood by Jessica's side, holding her right leg as she rested in between pushes. Then, oh my God, her head was out. I looked at CJ, who stood up by Jessica's head distancing himself from watching her birth up close.

My poor CJ! He was thrust into a situation that no one his age should have been in. I am certain that in his wildest imagination never would he have thought he would be part of a life-changing event such as this. Maybe for a baby entering the world under normal circumstances but not these.

The doctors suctioned Athena's nose and mouth and after doing so, told Jessica to push hard one more time. With the next surge, Athena's body was expelled with such force that amniotic fluid gushed onto my pants and open-toed sandals. I could feel her fluid on my feet, and as strange as it may sound, I felt baptized by her life and blessed by the miracle of her birth.

The NIC team quickly intercepted Athena and with urgency took her to her bassinet to assess her. Jessica had asked beforehand if she would be able to hold her baby, and it was not promised. Many mothers don't get to hold their babies when they are born, mainly when they are born by C-section. But this was different. Not only would Jessica not get to hold her baby, she didn't even get a glimpse of her. She would not be able to hold her daughter for many long days to come.

The energy in the room was intense and the room was crowded. CJ and I squeezed our way over to see her, as the doctors and nurses huddled tightly around her bassinet conducting their examination. The miracle that we had been waiting for what seemed like an eternity, our Athena, was finally here.

I thought that she would be in critical condition the moment she was born but she wasn't. I didn't understand how, the two main arteries of her heart being in the wrong position did not require immediate surgical intervention, but they didn't. After her initial evaluation she was quickly taken away to the NIC unit, which was just a few doors down the hall. CJ and I remained with Jessica while she recovered from her delivery, and we were all busy on our cell phones letting everyone know that she was here! Just like a chain letter, those phone calls sparked more calls. From California to Hawaii, the news traveled fast and our phones started ringing off the hook. Everyone, everyone, was so very, very happy.

People have described me as a fighter – fighting for good causes with a heart of justice, someone you'd want to have in your corner when things go wrong. After Jessica's recovery, she was moved into a room with another mother who had also just given birth. Jessica's bed was furthest from the door and we finally got her settled in. Not long after, people started flooding into the room to visit her roommate – lots of them. Their laughter and blissful excitement about their baby was rightfully deserved in any other circumstance. But our circumstances were never remotely normal, and I cringed over my daughter having to hear their conversations. Flowers, balloons and jubilant laughter filled their side of the room. Another event that was just too much to see my daughter be part of. Here, just hours before, she had given birth to a baby whom she wasn't allowed to see or hold, a baby that was in the Neonatal Intensive Care unit and would soon be undergoing heart surgery. Once again my heart ached for her. I soon after left the room, having to walk past the merriment and laughter of the visitors. Our eyes met and smiles were exchanged as I exited. Little did they know that in the midst of their celebration, the girl in the next bed hadn't yet seen or held her baby.

I walked to the nurse's station and asked for the head nurse. I explained our situation and asked if they could move my daughter to another room. She seemed sensitive to our circumstances and said she would do her best to find one for her. It didn't happen as quickly as I would have liked – a few hours – but she was moved down hall, around the corner, into a private room. I was thankful for the privacy, as this was not the time to be sharing space with anyone. Although Athena was here, there was unrest in our spirits, and we were still on edge. This is when we felt the impact of being so far from home. It was hard enough not having our family there for the birth of Athena, but to now face her surgery without our loved ones close by left a void in all three of us.

Later that afternoon, I would start to experience the two's-company-and three's-a-crowd syndrome. It had been Jessica, CJ and I for so long now, together all of the time. From the time we learned of Athena's condition, everywhere Jessica went I was with her. It didn't seem right that anyone would now try to separate our team. But in the NIC unit, only two people were allowed in at the same time, and so I had to wait outside in the hallway while Jess and CJ went in to see her for the first time. I know it made Jessica uncomfortable, too, but there was nothing we could do about it.

After a long and laborious wait, Jess and CJ walked out into the hallway and it was now – at last – my turn to see her. My heart was beating so fast while I sat there waiting. From the hallway I could see into the NIC unit and it was overwhelming to see the high tech machinery and all of the babies inside. Although it was a critical place for a baby to be, it actually looked calm and peaceful. The nurses all had the countenance of angels and the only part of their apparel that was missing from their sweet looking nursery scrubs, were their wings.

Here I was standing over the infant care bed, the third from the door, finally getting my first close up look of this little angel now here on earth. The one who'd I place my hands on her mother's stomach time and time again and feel her kick. The one whose face I was already familiar with by seeing her photos on the ultrasounds. The one whom I prayed on my knees for, the one who I rallied for – the one I joyfully and wholeheartedly dedicated my life to, traveling to another state to be there for her birth – the daughter of my daughter! I could hardly believe it! After everything that we'd been through, here now, in person, was our vision of love.

She had her daddy's nose and her mommy's big eyes and full lips. She looked peaceful wearing only a tiny diaper and a little beanie. The only medical intervention she had at the time was a PICC line running into her belly button. She wore a blood pressure cuff and a device to monitor her oxygen level. Even though she looked well, she wasn't. I thought about her little heart, how it seemed like it was beating like every other little baby's heart in that room, but it didn't. It was unnatural to see her just lying there. She should have been in her mother's arms, being kissed by her parents, sucking on her mother's breast. But she was not allowed to be held or fed, as she was being monitored around the clock for her impending surgery.

Jessica and CJ finally got settled into her new private room, Jess in her hospital bed and CJ on the roll away. When it came time for me to head back to the Ronald McDonald

House, I had a terrible feeling of separation anxiety. We had been together every night since we arrived in California, and that night I would be leaving my daughter and CJ for the first time. As soon as I closed the hospital room door behind me, I felt emptiness as large as the ocean that separated us from our home.

I found my way to the parking lot and got into my car. My wonderful, wonderful car, my only piece of home – the only form of familiarity in my life right then. I sat there for a few minutes with my face in my hands and cried. Happiness, exhaustion, apprehension, loneliness and worry for my daughter of what soon lie ahead.

The Ronald McDonald House was only a couple of minutes away. I parked my car in the underground parking lot and took the elevator up to the first floor, where the main living area was. I saw my Hispanic friend, who couldn't speak English. Our eyes met, and she made the motion of a pregnant stomach, asking about my daughter. I didn't know how else to tell her that she had given birth. So, like the game charades, I took both of my hands and gestured them between my legs and making the motion of something coming out, smiling at the thought of how ridiculous I must have looked. She knew exactly what I was saying, and we both laughed and hugged with happiness. I will never forget this special friend of mine.

I talked to Jessica a few times before I finally lay down. I spent the better part of the night making phone calls and talking to Ron. It was just still so unbelievable that Athena was here. I had a restless sleep that night as all I could think about was getting back to the hospital.

The next morning, I got to the hospital early and when I arrived there, Jessica wasn't in her room. I walked over to the hallway of the NIC unit and texted her. When she came out she told me that a surgery that morning had been cancelled and that Athena would be placed in that slot. Even though I knew the surgery would be soon, I wasn't prepared to hear this. Out of all of the days, weeks and months, and including the day she was born, this was the most intense day that was before us. I was suddenly overcome with emotion but once again I put a straight face and kept a brave front for the kids. I was the adult here, but honestly, inside I felt like a scared child.

I visited with Athena for a while and looked at this precious newborn citizen of our universe. I held her little hand and stroked her cheek. I talked to her and told her that I was her mommy's mommy and that I loved her. That I wrote a song for her and would play it for her on my piano when we got back home. It was gut wrenching knowing what she would soon be facing. Dear God, I know we've been preparing for this day, but how will we get through it? I thought. Please make this all just a bad dream and let me wake up.

Before she was whisked away, I asked the nurse if all three of us could be in the room at the same time so that we could pray for her before she went into surgery. While I was praying, I saw tears running down Jessica's cheeks and CJ's eyes welling with tears. If my heart ached any more than it already did for them at that moment, it would have broken. After we prayed, I left the room and waited outside while Athena's parents spent their last few moments with her.

When Athena was rolled out of the NIC unit in her bassinet with her parents and nurses alongside of her, I can't even describe the feeling. From the second a child is born, protectiveness for that child is immediately instilled in the parents and grandparents. How could we allow this to happen? The surgery was required to save her life, but to watch them roll her down that long hallway, to face this brutal surgery, was just too much to bear. We all said our goodbyes to Athena at the end of the hallway and gave her kisses. Then she was taken through those double doors while we stood there in silence, struggling to hold ourselves together.

Jessica and CJ tried their best to keep busy throughout the day even though there wasn't much for them to do. Jessica was still in her private room, and we spent most of our day there. Stanford had a beautiful cafeteria that we went to a couple of times to sit in the bright busy room. People came from all over the United States and in some cases, from out of the country to seek medical attention at this facility. I'd find myself looking at people and wondering what their story was and why they were there. I knew that there were many other people facing critical situations, and I often wished I could have talked to them, just to hear their stories.

Athena left for surgery in the late morning, and we were told that the procedure would take about six to seven hours. We knew that the preparation alone would take a quite a while as well, so we didn't really know how long it would be until we'd be able to see her again.

Seven o'clock that evening came after what seemed like an eternity, and there was still no word. After looking back on this day, I wondered why we weren't regularly updated on the progress of her surgery. No one should ever have to wait that long to find out what is going on with any lengthy surgery – let alone a critical one.

At around 10 p.m., we got the call that Athena was in the Cardiovascular Intensive Care Unit and that we could see her in about a half an hour. I swear, the furniture in the room could have moved from the exhale of our relief.

Still, I knew this part was going to be extremely hard on Jessica, and there was no way I could prepare her for what she was about to see. CJ, Jess and I found our way up to the CVICU unit, a specialized wing of the hospital that cares for patients with conditions ranging from myocardial infarctions and coronary interventions to heart failure and heart transplants.

We stood outside of the big electronic double doors that grandly opened to let us through once we were given permission to enter. Once inside, there was a large trough-type sink with foot pedals and soap dispensers where we stopped to scrub our hands and arms before proceeding any further. Once we were finished, we walked down the long, bright florescent-lit hallway in uncertainty, not knowing where to go. We walked to an area where the nurses and doctors were congregated – where it looked more like a busy morning rather than closing in on the midnight hour. The lead surgeon who performed this life saving surgery walked over to greet us and said that the surgery went well but that it was more complicated than he anticipated. He went on explaining why the surgery was more complex, but his words were a just a blur. We didn't need to understand the fine details at that moment. All we needed to know was that she made it, and we wanted to see her as soon as possible.

Every room in the CVICU is private with large plate glass windows so that the staff can see in. The patients, ranging from babies to the elderly, while in the critical stage, each have a nurse assigned to their rooms 24/7. When we got to the doorway where Athena lay, Jessica froze, literally stopping in her tracks and did not move. She folded her arms close to her body and stood outside the door staring at the baby that she had just delivered the day before. I stood close to her and motioned her to go in but she wouldn't. I continued to coax her into the room, but she did not budge.

I find it literally amazing what us mothers must and can do in moments of adversity. I kept finding strength within myself that I never could have imagined possessing. The protection I felt for my daughter at that moment completely overshadowed my own uneasiness. Jessica was the youngest of my three children, and she still felt like a child to me. Even now she still had the face of a 16 year old. How could I be standing here, watching my daughter have to face something that the most seasoned parent or mature adult would have a hard time coping with? I looked at her face and could see that she was visibly shaken. The core of my being ached for her, and I could barely hold back my tears. Another one of those, "Why God?" moments. Why does my daughter have to walk through this? What is she, what are we, supposed to learn from this experience? They say that God never gives you more than you can handle, but at that moment I didn't believe that he'd purposefully lay this on an innocent 22-year-old girl. She didn't have enough life experience of her own to go through this let alone learn something from it. Why should anyone have to handle this? God only knows I didn't want to handle it. I agonized over my daughter having to see her daughter this way.

I tried my best to get her into the room, but I eventually had to stop. I knew that as much as she wanted to, she couldn't bring herself to see her baby up close. The room alone was intimidating with all of the specialized machines. Jessica and CJ remained just outside the door while I went in.

Athena was in an induced coma and on a ventilator with tape running across her mouth to hold the tube in place. Her chest was bandaged from her collarbone to her belly. Tubes and lines seemed to be attached to her everywhere – connected to the most high tech machinery imaginable. Her little hands were each strapped to boards preventing her from moving them. It was heart wrenching. We were reassured by her attending nurse that she was not in any pain and that she was doing extremely well and in stable condition. We didn't stay there too long as Jessica wanted to go back to her room. Once getting back there, I stayed with her and CJ for a while, doing my best to reassure them that the worst part was now behind Athena, and for all of us.

I had to leave her again for another night and it was even harder than the one before. She had CJ, the love of her life with her but, even with him there, I knew that she needed me, too. I wish I could have picked her up, sat down on the rocking chair with her, and held her close to me. I just didn't want to go. Jessica would not only not cry, she wouldn't even let me embrace her. To this day, I am not sure why Jessica displays such a lack of emotion. Maybe because I've always been so sentimental and she didn't want to be like me. I've always tried to get it across to Jessica that crying was not a sign of weakness; as a matter of fact, it was just the opposite. My sister once said to me, which made a lot of sense, that tears come from a place of truth and love, which I always held to be true. I suspected that Jessica felt that she had to be strong for CJ, so she kept that stiff upper lip of hers even tighter than ever. But at a time when I wanted to just hold her and cry for all of us, she wouldn't let me.

I returned to the hospital the next morning just before 7 a.m., Jess told me that after I left, they went up to see Athena and stayed with her for a long time. She went on to say that the nurses went over everything with her and CJ, and I felt so relieved knowing that Jessica faced her fears and was able to see her child. The three of us then made our way back to the CVICU to see her.

Jessica was discharged from the hospital the next day and here we were, experiencing yet another adversity – Jessica having to leave the hospital without her baby. But she had no choice and did what she had become accustomed to – doing what she didn't want but had to do. She had already begun the task of pumping her breast milk to store for Athena for when she'd be able to drink it. I was so proud of how diligent she was at pumping. Because she couldn't yet be with her baby, she was doing what she could for her and it gave her purpose.

Over the next two days, Athena progressed well and was quickly off the ventilator. The time finally arrived when Jessica was going to be able to hold her for the first time and I couldn't wait! I knew what it felt like to hold my child for the first time, and I could not imagine how she felt having to wait this long to hold her. I instantly felt Jessica's joy the moment Athena was placed in her arms. She looked blissful that morning, and the expression on her face when she held her was something I will never forget. Mother and child at last. At last.

My husband and I talked often, having more than several long conversations each day. Now that the surgery was over and Athena was well on her way to recovery, he prepared for his absence from our company and purchased his ticket to come see her. He told me that our son would also be coming the day after him, and I was thrilled with this unexpected news. Matthew also had a job that was difficult for him to leave and a family of his own. But that was my son, tender-hearted just like his father, loving his sister enough to make the journey across the ocean to see her and her baby. My middle child, Kendra, stayed back to watch our home and to take care of my dogs now that Ron would be gone. A sacrifice she made, to this day, that still haunts her. She never got to meet her sister's child, her beloved niece. This did not only break her heart, but it later caused her to sink into a deep, understandable depression.

Every morning of the week that Athena was in the CVICU, I'd wake up at the Ronald McDonald House around 5 a.m., get dressed, and walk downstairs to the kitchen. I'd make my cup of coffee in one of those machines where you'd pop a single little container of coffee into it that brewed one perfect cup. I loved the feeling of the morning, seeing the familiar family faces strolling into the kitchen with the promise of the new day ahead of them. Even though we hadn't been at the Ronald McDonald House very long, I had already established a strong connection with several of the families there. We were all so very different, from all over the country, but we had one thing very much in common. We were all there for someone we loved and to lend support to one another. There were many unspoken words in that house, but so well understood by one another.

After my coffee, I'd take the elevator to the garage, excited to feel the cold air once I reached my car. I'd drive to the hospital and always arrive before 6 a.m. As I did every day, I'd check in with the security guard and was asked the same important question while showing my identification. Where I was going and if I had any signs of a cold or sickness. The hospital was vigilant about keeping sick visitors at bay as so many critical patients were hospitalized there. Once I was cleared, a nametag would be written out and handed to me. I placed it on my chest like a badge of honor and I was granted permission to enter the hospital. I'd board the elevator up to the third floor and, once informing the nurse's station I was there, be let in by the automatic doors of the CIVICU unit. I'd stop to scrub my hands and arms topped off by running my hands under a censored dispenser that would drop a small amount of antibacterial gel on my hands and rub them together until they were dry. We all took the ritual of washing of our hands very seriously. Everyone in that unit was in a vulnerable state, and germs were a big threat.

As I approached her room, I could see her through the glass window, in her little bassinet, seeing that little crop of dark hair first. On the second morning after her surgery, one of the nurses had made a bright pink sign with Athena's name in big black letters that she placed on top of her cubicle. It felt so surreal to see her name there like that. I thought about the song I wrote for her while she was still growing within her mother and what the name Athena meant then, compared to what it meant now. Sweet, sweet little Athena Marie. A new branch of our family tree that made our lives so much more worth living for. I always had to stop myself from crying before going in to see her. Seeing her lying there like that was unnatural and depressing. As soon as I entered her room, I was greeted by the nurse on duty that filled me in with her progress. Every day it only got better and better, and she never had any setbacks.

How I treasured this time with my granddaughter. When I'd first see her, I always greeted her in the tune of a song, singing, "I'm your Mommy's Mommy! "

Athena's eyes were big, dark and intense. She'd listen with her eyes and stare at my face. She gripped my finger as I touched her hand and nothing else in the world mattered during that time with her. I talked to her, sang to her, and told her stories about her mom. To not be able to hold her was maddening. I said a lot to her during those early morning hours, but had I had known our time together would be so short, I would have said a whole lot more. Jessica and CJ would let me have those first couple of hours with her before they came. Once there, I'd let them have their private time with Athena before returning to her room around twelve.

My husband and I talked, both about Jessica, the baby and work. As odd as it sounds, even with all that was going on, I still continued to log into my office in Hawaii and edit the investigations once they were completed. This is one area that I trusted no one else with during my absence. I had been editing our reports for more than 25 years and knew I had to manage this part of my job while I was away, no matter what.

The day Ron told me he had made his reservation to come see the baby, I was overjoyed. A month had passed since I had seen him, and I relentlessly felt his absence. From drinking our coffee together in the morning till kissing him goodnight, we were extremely close and did everything together.

I can still remember the day he arrived at the Ronald McDonald House in a shuttle bus taken from the airport after landing in California. If ever there was a love scene from the movie of my life, this was definitely one of the more significant ones. It was late at night, and the house was quiet with most of the families settled into their quarters. Diffused lights illuminated the hallways and there was such peacefulness about the place in light of the struggles that lay behind all of the closed doors. The main floor of the house was beautiful. Looking back now, I realize that the reason why it felt so amazing was because of the people who worked there and the families who took up residence within it. Not only did the first floor accommodate the reception area, the kitchen and dining area, laundry room, TV room, and library, it also had a grand sitting area with 30-foot-high ceilings with tall glass windows looking out to the courtyard. It was exquisite. The kitchen lights were dimmed with a few restless people straggling in and out. But for the most part, it was just me, Jess and CJ, waiting for Ron to arrive. There was a turnaround area in front of the house where the shuttle bus would arrive. I was so excited while waiting for him I couldn't stop pacing.

The bus finally arrived, and my heart pounded as I saw its headlights circling around the bend of the driveway. Seeing Ron for the first time, stepping out of the bus was a sight to behold. He looked so handsome with his dark slacks, a light-colored sports jacket, and a Hawaiian Kukui nut lei draped around his neck. I embraced him like a lost child reunited with her parent. God, I was happy! My safety net, my life partner, my husband had arrived. I felt weakened by the adrenaline pumping through my body while waiting for him. After all of our hugs and kisses we gave him a short tour of the house. I was eager to show him our new home, while away from ours.

I was used to sleeping in the same room with Jessica and CJ by now and was familiar with all of their habits. Jess would normally fall asleep early while CJ watched TV late into the night. It felt slightly awkward now with the four of us there. Poor Ron. I only had a twin bed and we both couldn't fit in it. So, he slept on the floor on the airbed that the maintenance man brought up when I told them he was coming. When I woke up early in the morning, I saw that his bed had deflated to the point where he was sleeping on the hard floor. I asked him to switch places with me, but being the gentleman that he has been from the first day I met him, he stayed right where he was. I woke up again several times that night just to look at him and I couldn't believe that he was really there.

We both got up early the next morning. He was still on Hawaiian time, which we were three hours ahead of. I knew he was exhausted, but we both couldn't wait to get to the hospital. We got dressed and went downstairs to the kitchen where I made us both a cup of coffee. I felt wonderful having the people who had seen me alone all this time to now to see my husband with me. We drank our coffee quickly as I couldn't wait a minute longer to introduce him to our brand new baby granddaughter.

We took the elevator down to my car, and I must say, it felt really strange to get into it with him. Here we were, both in California, in another state, not at work like we usually were, getting into my car to drive to the hospital to see our newborn granddaughter that just had underwent heart surgery. I often had to pinch myself to make sure that I wasn't dreaming.

We arrived there in just a few minutes. As I approached it, I just loved looking at the building and thinking Athena was there and being well taken care of. This was a place where lives were saved, where miracles occurred. I will forever be grateful for this institution.

We entered the CVICU, and the staff already knew me. But this was Ron's first time there, and I handed the nurse a note I had written and had Jessica sign, giving him permission to visit Athena. After he passed the security of the nurse's station, we walked into her room, holding hands.

I was struck with the memories of holding his hand when I was only 22 and how madly in love I was with him. And now, at 58 years old, with all that we had been through and what we were facing at this moment, I reflected on all the years that had past us by. What I had perceived as love in my youth was nothing compared to the level of love I felt for him on that day he would meet Athena. I remembered the innocence of our lives back then and now, here we were, entering the room of our granddaughter, the daughter of our daughter, the granddaughter who had just been born and went through heart surgery. I believe this one the most profound moment of our lives together, and our love became even stronger at this very moment in time.

I still have the picture on our bookcase that I had one of the nurses take of us that morning – each of us standing on opposite sides of Athena's bassinet, holding hands over her. There is so many times that when I think back on such moments that I just want to evaporate, to literally vanish from my life. To have gone from falling in love with this precious, innocent baby, only to have her taken from us. When your own children are little and even when they are grown, you know that having your children go before you is un-natural and you wonder how anyone could deal with the loss of their child. But not once, not once, did I ever think of this of happening to our own child.

The very next day, Matthew arrived at the hospital. It was so amazing to me to think that my grown son, my first born, whom I literally didn't put down for the first year of his life, flew clear across the Pacific Ocean from Hawaii to California, rented a car, checked into a motel, and found his way to the hospital. It was like a dream seeing him, and I felt an even deeper sense of security with him there. He loved his sister and sacrificed so much to be with her. What an adoring soul he was. We met in the cafeteria and ate some lunch together before we went upstairs and introduced Athena to her Uncle Matt.

The day before Matthew arrived; Athena was moved from the CVICU to another unit, on the third floor, called Three West. She was doing so well that she longer required the care of a personal nurse. Jessica and CJ were now allowed to live in her room with her so she was never alone. She still had a feeding tube inserted through her nose, as she was not quite getting the hang of nursing or being bottle fed yet. She went one full week after she was born with not eating and therefore needed to learn how to suckle. Surprisingly, it didn't come as easy as I thought it would. It was interesting how the nurses monitored how much breast milk she was taking in by weighing her diapers. Jessica continued to pump her milk, like a dairy factory, to store up her baby's nourishment. I knew she was frustrated with not being able to nurse, and pumping her breast milk was the only thing she felt she could do for her baby before she really latched on.

With the three of us there and knowing she'd be in good hands, Jessica asked us if we'd watch over Athena for a while so that she and CJ could go back to the Ronald McDonald House to wash up and get a little rest. Ron, Matthew and I joyfully spent the entire day with her, taking turns holding her and texting pictures to family. She was dressed in a little red Hawaiian outfit that a nurse, who was born and raised in Hawaii, had made for her. As I type these words, I am looking at a picture I took of my son with Athena on this day. The smile on his face expressed exactly how the three of us felt with her – blissful.

Ron and I decided to stay in motel a short distance away from the hospital so that we could sleep comfortably together. Matthew also rented a room at the same motel with us on the top floor and he on the ground. That night, we took Matthew out to dinner at a seafood restaurant in lovely Palo Alto. After our son graduated from high school, he left home at 18, to go to college in California. He moved back home for a short period of time before getting married at the young age of 20. Over the years, we spent time together at family dinners and holidays, but we rarely spent any one-on-one time with him. And here we were, sitting in this romantic, dimly lit posh restaurant, with people finely dressed, candles on each table, just me and my husband and our son. Athena was finally here, her surgery was over, and not only was my husband with me, but my son too! It felt wonderful just to sit there with the two most important men in my life. I had a glass of wine and basked in our time together. My heart felt full that evening.

Matthew was only able to stay a few days and it was hard to see him go. But he had to get back to work and we knew it wouldn't be long until we'd all be together again. We were already planning a homecoming party for Athena with our family. Athena was doing well, and he left on a positive note. What a wonderful big brother he was to both of his sisters. Matthew excelled at everything he did in life and was the epitome of a big brother. The last day he was with us in Athena's hospital room, he showed Jessica how to change a diaper. It was a light and playful scene that only a mother could appreciate – a true Kodak moment...With three children of his own, Matthew was a seasoned parent and a natural at changing diapers.

CJ's parents and sister arrived in town a day or two after Ron did. Now that they were here too, Ron and I decided to venture out on our own for a day, to spend some long, overdue time together. It was my first time away from the hospital, and although I was happy to be with my husband, I felt uneasy leaving Jessica, CJ and the baby behind.

From our room at the Ronald McDonald House, the kids and I would always hear the sound of a train running through the town and it sounded so romantic to me. As a child, I took a train trip with my mother from California to Nebraska and had wonderful memories of it. I Googled information about the Palo Alto train and learned that a station was located nearby and that it traveled to San Francisco – the place of my birth! We decided that we would check it out and punched the address into my car's GPS and was guided to the terminal. The train was another thing that we didn't have back home, and it was a novelty to be able to ride it. I felt like a kid as we sat in our seats looking out the window as we moved along the different cities. It was fun just sitting there, relaxing to the movement of the train. It felt good to let go and to let my mind wander. I was relaxed, and with my husband now with me, I felt at peace.

We got off the train near downtown Market Street in San Francisco. You may as well have dropped us into another place in the world, as it felt so drastically different from home. The sky was gray, and people hurried along the sidewalks dressed in their winter wardrobes.

I moved to Hawaii when I was 18 and lived there all of my adult life. I had adapted to its culture and even married into it. The difference between Hawaii and California is truly like night and day. Just the way people were dressed was a huge contrast. Back home, people dressed light and casual. Here, everyone was covered up with coats. After we got off the train, we stopped to put our jackets on, as it was cold. But I loved the feeling. It was energizing – much more comfortable than the Hawaiian humidity. We found our way to a Starbucks and sat down to a tall cup of Americano, a favorite of ours. We didn't spend much down time back home, as we were always hard pressed for time with our business and family responsibilities. Relaxation really wasn't part of our lifestyle, especially this past six months with all that had been going on with Jessica. What a wonderful feeling, sitting in the warmth of the café, just being together. It almost felt like we were young and carefree again without a worry in the world.

After we left Starbucks, we walked along Market Street and ended up in one of my favorite stores – Ross! Of all the things we could do, we spent about an hour shopping there. I loved looking at sweaters and clothing that I knew I could only wear while in California. But I loved my new California wardrobe of leggings and long sweaters, at least for the time being.

We walked around and window shopped a couple of more hours then decided to have lunch before heading back to the train station. Along the way back to the terminal, we found an Indian restaurant and had lunch there. The food was so delicious that I made Ron promise me that one day after we were back home and life was back to normal again, we'd return to San Francisco one day just to eat at this same restaurant.

Ron was only able to stay for a little over a week, and the time passed quickly. We spent all of our mornings with Athena. Now that she was moved into her own room and out of critical care, CJ and Jess were able to stay with her while Ron and I moved back into the Ronald McDonald House. Thanksgiving was coming up, and numerous volunteers brought meals to the house. I think they made about three Thanksgiving dinners in all, two during the week and one on Thanksgiving Day. Some of the volunteers brought all of their own ingredients and cooked the turkeys' right there in the kitchen. The aroma of the turkeys cooking in the ovens permeated the house with a warm feeling of comfort that temporarily eased our weary souls.

Jessica and CJ would come back to the house in the evenings, to eat, shower and grab whatever they needed before returning back to the hospital.

On Thanksgiving Day, after waking up especially early, Ron said, "Let's go visit your mom and sister." They lived in Northern California, about three hours away from the hospital, and driving there sounded totally absurd to me. I wasn't the kind of person who could just pick up on a whim and go somewhere. I was a planner, and this definitely wasn't in my plans. For over a half an hour he tried convincing me why we should go, with me resisting every step of the way. CJ's parents were still in town, and I knew Jessica and CJ would be okay with us being gone. I had separation anxiety when away from Jessica, but Ron made his case, and the verdict was in: We were going! My sister was just about to start her chemotherapy treatments, and if ever there was a reason to visit them, this certainly was it. So, off we went in my car with our GPS leading the way. I felt relieved with Ron driving, but I still felt apprehensive knowing that we'd soon have to cross the Bay Bridge. While driving over it, I told him how scared I felt and asked him to sing to me. I was taken aback when he started singing "London Bridge is Falling Down." If he weren't driving, I would have punched him in his arm. That wasn't funny.

I was overjoyed seeing my family in rustic Grass Valley, California. It was a magical experience for us to take in the beautiful scenery of late autumn in this rural part of the country. The trees were unbelievable. Yes, Hawaii is paradise, but California has a beauty all of its own that I so loved. Once we were there and settled in with a glass of wine, I showed them all of my pictures of Athena. There was no denying that I was a proud grandmother of my little warrior.

Athena is Released to the Ronald McDonald House

Just as we were about finished eating dinner, I got a text from Jessica saying that Athena had been released from the hospital. What? I can't even begin to express my angst when reading this message. Who in the world lets a patient out of the hospital on Thanksgiving Day? Her release was a landmark occasion – an event I wouldn't have missed for anything – and now, here I was, three long hours away from the hospital and unable to be part of her "homecoming" to the Ronald McDonald House. My sister having breast cancer rocked me, and I was happy to spend time with both her and my mom, yet, I was going to be absent for this long awaited, momentous occasion. I was so upset about missing her release, but there was nothing I could do about it.

We spent the night at my mom's house that night, and I felt happy to be with her again. The temperature was in the 40's and she turned the heater on, something that I had a hard time adjusting to when in California. Back home, our windows are open just about every day of the year, and the combination of the artificial heat and the closed windows made me feel slightly claustrophobic. But after a long night full of chatting, we fell asleep to the heater's hum.

As soon as I woke up, I could barely contain my energy as I had one focus and one focus only – to get back to Palo Alto to my granddaughter who was now at the Ronald McDonald

House. Being that Stanford was only a few minutes away; she was released from the hospital but not discharged from care. A follow up appointment was already in place for her in one week.

To leave my mother that morning was bittersweet. At the delicate age of 85, every time I said goodbye to her over the telephone while in Hawaii, or now, in person, I always had that dreaded feeling of "what if?" What if this is the last time I hear her voice? What if this is the last time I will see her, I wondered. Even though she was in the best of health, you just never knew. I had a hard time leaving, but we had to go. I can still remember my mom's face when I was 18 and leaving home, suitcase in hand, with her insisting that I not go. It was only after I became a mother did I understand the full impact of what she must have felt that day. Deep down inside, I always felt guilty for living in Hawaii all these years. I knew she would have rather had me close by and not an ocean separating us. Driving away from her, watching her wave goodbye until I couldn't see her any longer was so painful, tears trickled down my checks for the first half hour of our drive back to Palo Alto.

What an amazing feeling it was, to return to our room at the Ronald McDonald House and see Athena there. I was completely overwhelmed with emotion when I walked through the door and saw her. To have seen her in the Cardiovascular Intensive Care Unit with lines running in and out of her in every which way and then to see her in a home environment, I was taken aback and fought hard to hold back the tears. The Ronald McDonald House provided a beautiful soft white bassinet for her to sleep in for the remainder of our stay. Seeing her like this provided a feeling of normalcy, that, yes, she was born with a heart problem, but they fixed it, and now, we could move forward. To soon bring her home, introduce her to our family, to love her, to raise her. At this point, we didn't know what her limitations or restrictions would be in the future, but it didn't matter right now. She was out of the hospital, and we were one step closer to going home.

My husband had to leave the next day, and we spent our last night at the hotel together. I was so restless with the thought of him leaving and woke up so many times that night. Each time I awoke I'd look at him – trying to soak in his presence so that after he was gone, I'd still feel him with me. I didn't know how much longer we would be in California and now that he was here, I didn't want to be without him again. I slept close to him that night and every time I woke up, I'd listen to the rhythm of his heartbeat and drift back off to sleep.

The alarm clock unsympathetically woke us at 4:15 am. I laid there watching him get ready with just the dressing room light on, feeling a sense of dread. At 5 a.m., we walked outside, down the stairs and to the street where the shuttle bus was already waiting for him, steam from the exhaust trailing out from the pipe. I held onto him like a child not wanting to let go of their parent on the first day of school. I tried my best to be strong – I didn't want him to feel any worse than he already did about having to leave me. But our company couldn't withstand his absence much longer, and he had to return to Hawaii. After I kissed him one more time, he entered the side sliding door, and the driver zoomed off in a hurry. I stood out on the street watching the van until I couldn't see it any longer and slowly walked back upstairs to our room. Once I closed and locked the door behind me, I immediately felt that emptiness again. I lay down for a little while knowing that I'd talk to him again before he boarded his flight and drifted back off to sleep.

I woke up at 6:30 a.m., and after talking to Ron before his plane took off, I made my mind up that I would not dwell on him leaving. I decided that I would cook dinner at the Ronald McDonald House for Jessica, CJ and his family that day to keep busy. I was excited to get back to the house and to be able to stay back in the room with Jessica, CJ, and our beloved Athena Marie.

At 8:30 a.m., I was all packed up and rolled my suitcase down the stairs, meeting up with my dear car once again. As soon as I sat down in it, I said to myself, "You can do this!"

I'd become accustomed to doing so much on my own now and was starting to adjust to it better. It was cold outside, which I normally love, but now that Ron had left, I felt a mean chill running through my body.

Once leaving the hotel, I headed straight for Safeway to grocery shop. I decided to make a pot of my famous shoyu chicken for dinner which Jessica and CJ both loved. Because it was still so early in the morning, I took my time shopping for all of the ingredients. Back home, I was always in a rush, and I never felt relaxed in the supermarket. But here I was, able to take my time, and I enjoyed it. I swear, sometimes I felt like someone with a double identity. As I pushed my shopping cart up and down the aisles, I'd smile at other shoppers. I'm certain that I didn't look any different from anyone else, but I felt like I was in disguise as this was not my real life.

I was grateful that my husband was able to provide for us the way that he did during our time in California, as the expense of our trip was enormous. Anything we needed and the little extras to make things more comfortable for us, I was able to purchase. He made a lot of sacrifices for us to be there, taking on the entire financial responsibility of our journey, running our company without me and maintaining our home. It was a lot for him. But I knew that he loved taking care of us – all of us, including CJ and our granddaughter, Athena.

I just loved the underground parking lot of the Ronald McDonald House. The cement walls kept the basement at a refrigerator like temperature, and as soon as I opened the door of my car, the cold invigorated me. I took the elevator up to the main floor of the house, put away the groceries, and crept into the room, only to find everyone still asleep. Athena was sleeping with her mommy, tucked in right next to her shoulder, and the world could not have looked any more beautiful than it did to me that morning, in light of Ron now in the air, heading back home.

Later in the morning Jessica told me that CJ's parent's wanted to take her, CJ and the baby out and asked me if I wanted to come along. I knew she didn't want to leave me by myself but I politely declined as I just wanted to stay back at the house to cook, tidy up our room, and relax. It turned out to be a long day, as they didn't get back until 8:30 p.m. I spent a lot of time in the kitchen, standing vigil over my industrial-sized pot of shoyu chicken, simmering to perfection. A couple that we became fond of, Jason and Sonia, found their way to the island I was cooking on, by the aroma of the savory mixture of soy sauce, brown sugar, ginger and garlic. Jason sampled the chicken I had been laboring over all day, and he loved it. That Jason, he was quite a character. He was an entrepreneur and a mathematical wizard. He tutored Jessica on how to achieve a good credit score at a young age, and helped a little girl, whose sister had a heart transplant, with her math homework. The kitchen became such an important place to many of us. It was our sanctuary, a place where we'd meet, talk and try to incorporate normalcy into our lives as we struggled to deal with our individual challenges. Jason and Sonia had an infant daughter, Ariana, who also underwent heart surgery followed by major complications.

As soon as Jess, CJ and his family returned with Athena, I served dinner right away, as it was late and I was beat. While we were all sitting around the dining room table, Jessica quietly showed me Athena's incision and told me that she thought it looked a little red. It alarmed me, and I told her that she needed to take her to the hospital and have her looked at, which she agreed.

Everyone was tired by this time, and once we finished with dinner CJ's family left for their hotel. All I can say is thank God for the Ronald McDonald House. The hospital was practically right around the corner, and we felt reassured knowing that help was always a matter of minutes away. Jess and CJ took Athena to the hospital to have her looked at while I stayed in our room, worrying about her.

They returned, with Athena, a little after 2 a.m., and told me there was no infection. We were relieved and went to sleep soon after. Athena was on several medications and had to take the refrigerated one every six hours. Jess got up at 6 a.m., like clockwork and went downstairs to the kitchen to retrieve her morning medicine from the refrigerator.

CJ's family had another event planned that day, and Jess asked me if I would watch her as she thought it would be too cold to take her out. I was over the moon with the thought of having her to myself for the day. Athena was breast-fed but also took it from the bottle. So, with instructions of medication at hand and an ample supply of breast milk in the fridge, off they went. This was my first day of having her all to me, and I was in heaven.

Jess and I talked off and on during the day and I texted her pictures of Athena. I know she felt nervous about leaving her, but she knew she was in good hands and trusted me completely. I was happy for her that she had a chance to get away. If anyone deserved a day to relax and enjoy themselves, it was Jessica. It has been a long time leading up to this day, when she could finally let go of her worries and have some fun.

Athena and I had a full day together. I fed her, rocked her, sang to her, and read her very first book to her, "I'll Love You Forever," one of our family favorites. When Jessica was a toddler, I caught her sitting on the toilet with tons of toilet paper stuffed into the bowl, just like the cover of the book. I grabbed my camera, took a picture of it, and eventually had it made into a poster. That picture hung on the wall of the bathroom for years, and everyone got the biggest kick out of it. As I was reading the ending of the book to her, I started to choke up, as the story is so tender hearted. I apologized to her, telling her that her grandma was a crybaby, but that I was only crying because I loved her so much. I swear she understood me as the look on her beautiful baby face just seemed to say, "I understand Grandma!" I am forever grateful for that day. This little living-breathing child that I loved profusely was here. It was just she and I and no day so far, had been better than this one.

Everything was going right, and our worries seemed to be behind us now. We just had a few more days to go until

Athena had her final checkup, and if everything looked good, she would be completely discharged from her care at Stanford, and we could start preparing for our return home to Hawaii. When we made our original flight plans, we had to pick a return date to take advantage of the round trip fares, knowing very well that we might have to change it. But our reservations were set for December 14, and it looked like the timing would work out perfectly. This would allow us to return to my mom's condo in Vallejo and spend time with my family, before our voyage back to our island of Oahu.

CJ's family left that weekend, and our final appointment for Athena was scheduled for December 1st. I could hardly believe that time was passing by so quickly now. Little by little, I started getting our things together wondering how we would be able to transport all of our belongings back to Mom's condo. Jess had bought a car seat/stroller combo while we were there and we now had to make some alternative plans to get us and our things back to Vallejo. My sweet sedan could no longer accommodate our newest addition and all of our belongings.

On December 1, Jess and CJ took Athena for her final visit at Stanford while I stayed back at the house packing up and cleaning our room. She had an echocardiogram that day, and the doctor said that all looked well with her heart.

I was in high spirits knowing that this leg of our journey was coming to an end but sad at the same time. I had become extremely attached to this new home of ours and to the many remarkable families we shared it with.

If ever there was a glimpse of heaven while on earth, I have seen it first hand at the Ronald McDonald House. It was like being in God's loving care, and I will never forget this place. But the time had come for us to get on with our lives and to say goodbye.

My brother Jimmy volunteered to help transport the overload of our belongings back to Moms' condo, while I drove us there.

After Athena's final doctor appointment, Jessica called me

to tell me that her checkup went well and that she was completely discharged from the hospital. After our conversation I felt that now familiar feeling of surrealness and could hardly believe that this chapter of our lives was coming to a close. I called my brother to let him know that Athena had been completely released from her care at Stanford and that we'd be finished packing up and ready to leave by the time he got there. It was about an hour and a half drive for him and that gave us ample time to finalize our exit.

After Jimmy arrived, I felt tremendous anxiety. Here we were, packing up our cars with all of our belongings, with Athena fully released to our sole custody. In a way, it almost felt like the day of her birth as her little life was governed by so many people up until this moment. Now there she was, bundled up in her car seat, ready to be placed in my car that sailed across the ocean for her, to transport her back to our real lives and start anew.

One of the last things we had to do at the Ronald McDonald House was to have a final room inspection and to return our identification badges that we wore around our necks at all times while in the house. Their security system was flawless with the safety of the families being their number one priority. We said our goodbyes, hugged so many people, and with tears in my eyes, I started the engine of my car and drove off.

I was still uncomfortable driving on the freeways, especially at night, and just as I suspected, it got dark towards the middle of our drive back to Moms. We were right behind Jimmy's car when we left but I knew that following someone for a long period of time was difficult. So, with the GPS on and now having a general sense of the direction of where we were headed, I drove on my own. Athena started to cry a couple of times during the drive back, and about three quarter of the way through, it started to rain. The roads were wet and dark, and this was the first time I was driving with her in the car. If there was ever a time that I felt more responsible for someone's safety, it was then. My body and eyes were fatigued, but I just pressed on and drove both offensively and defensively.

As we got closer to moms, I was familiar with the area, and I was beyond excited that we were almost there. There was a small shopping center a few minutes away from the condo, and I pulled into the parking lot of a small convenience store. I called Jimmy on his cell phone to tell him that we were going to make a quick stop at the store, and he said he was actually a few minutes behind us. Jessica stayed in the car with sleeping Athena while CJ and I went inside. CJ had bought some poke (raw fish) from L&L in Palo Alto before we left, and we were going to celebrate with our favorite delicacy, poke and beer, once we got there. I bought a small bottle of the best whiskey I could find so that my brother could join us in our milestone celebration. My nursing Jessica was merrily going to celebrate with fruit juice although I knew she would love nothing more than to have had a strawberry daiquiri.

I remember the first night we arrived at moms, after landing in California. There was a huge black iron security gate that mom had to electronically open from her unit to let us in. I felt humbled to be there and watched the gate slowly close behind us, securing us into our new home while away from ours, for now.

This night with Mom still in Grass Valley, we had to physically punch in the gate code ourselves. The feeling of it opening this time had a completely different sensation to it. That night, as it opened, it felt like the arms of an angel welcoming Athena home, and when closing, the promise of protecting her while she was there.

I felt like a child on Christmas morning getting back to the condo. Jimmy and CJ made several trips between both cars to bring in our luggage. The night was cold, lightly raining, and the complex was dark and quiet. The lampposts that bordered the walkways cast a subtle light on the beautiful trees and foliage that surrounded the place – simply picturesque.

Once we were settled in, we poured our drinks and huddled in a circle, clicking our beverages together in a chime of victory, while Athena lay peacefully sleeping. To stand there at that moment, to be back to where our journey in California began, with Athena now with us, was one of the most extraordinary moments of our lives. To think of what we had been through, what Athena had went through, and there we were, with her, safe and sound, preparing for our last stretch of this journey before returning home.

The next morning, CJ happily slept in while Jessica tended to Athena. She slept most of the day, waking only to nurse, be changed, and to take her medications. Jessica had always been a natural at everything she did and motherhood was no different. She was utterly in love with her baby, and you would have thought she already had children by the ease in which she cared for her. What a lucky baby she was to have Jessica for her mommy. Because she loved the outdoors so much, Jessica already had a list a mile long of all the things she and Athena would do as she grew. She already had a baby bikini for her as I'm sure, the ocean was first on the list, when Athena was able to go into the salt water.

The morning went by quickly and the only outing that day was my grocery shopping to stock up on supplies. We returned to the condo with Athena on December 1, and our flight home wasn't until the 14th. So for that reason, I needed to stock up our fridge and pantry once again with all the necessary staples and lots of our favorite snacks. CJ loved salami and Gouda cheese while Jessica loved saimin. Raley's Supermarket was my favorite grocery store to shop at, and I felt like a kid in a candy store whenever in there, especially in the lush produce section. I made their favorite dinner that night, hamburger steak, with a pot of rice and thick brown gravy.

Friday came before we knew it, and the morning started off much like the day before. Jessica was up early to give Athena her morning medicines, and took her back to sleep. I made my morning coffee and logged into my computer at work to check on what was happening there. We had a relaxing day and it felt good not having to go anywhere. We just stayed put and enjoyed Athena.

In the late afternoon, Athena started crying and Jessica had a difficult time trying to console her. I can still see Jessica rocking her back and forth in her arms trying to calm her. I felt alarmed by the way she was crying, as we had not really heard her cry very much up until then.

This is the day, the one day in my entire life that I would give anything to go back and do over again. This is the one day that I have agonized over to the point where I literally thought I would go mad. This is the one day that I harbored great guilt over and I was never really able to forgive myself for even though everyone told me I had to. This is the sole reason why I accompanied my daughter to the mainland, to love and protect her, and her baby. I was the mother, and I should have known better.

Jessica and I looked over the paperwork we were sent home with when Athena was fully discharged from Stanford, and we started reviewing all of the different literature. I found the section on baby's crying and read it out loud to Jessica. At that point, we thought she might be colicky. Even though I was extremely worried, I knew I had the tendency to overreact, and so I thought this was another time that I just needed to calm down and stop thinking the worst. Athena eventually stopped crying and we were relieved. I went to the store later in the day and bought a baby swing, thinking it might help soothe her. The rest of the evening went relatively well and Athena seemed to be okay. CJ put the swing together and she happily slept while it slowly rocked her back and forth.

The next day, was December 4th, and the countdown was on. We were only 10 days away from bringing Athena home, and as much as I looked forward to it, I was filled with mixed emotions about leaving.

I woke up early that morning feeling content knowing that Jessica, CJ and Athena were peacefully sleeping. I made my morning cup of coffee and sipped it at the kitchen table while logging in to my office computer. A little while later, Jessica came into the living area and asked if I could watch

Athena so that she could sleep a little longer.

I truly believe that God had placed me there for that very moment in time, and I will forever be grateful. "Of course I will," I said, while Jessica sleepily returned to her room. That morning I did what I always did when Athena was in my care. I didn't take my eyes off her. I talked to her, read to her, sang to her, changed her, and fed her. Held her. Loved her, loved her, loved her...

I was looking forward to going out for a while after Jessica got up so that I could look for a tub to bathe her in. At her last appointment, Jessica was told that she could now be submerged in water. We were looking forward to giving her a real bath as we had only been able to sponge bathe her up until now. Her incision was healing well, but it was still hard to look at. It was a reminder of what she had been through, but more importantly, I told myself, what she made it through.

Jessica got up at about noon and profusely thanked me for letting her get some extra rest. Once we discussed Athena's schedule that morning, what we did, how much breast milk she drank, and her medications, I put on my jacket and left to go shopping.

I felt excited to get out into the cold California air and looked forward to spending some time alone. As I started to drive away from the condo, I thought about how much I was going to miss it here. After all that we had been through it felt like we had put down some roots and as odd as it sounds, it started to feel like home. I was now able to get around without the GPS, and I was finally comfortable driving there. I shopped at several stores looking for a bathtub for Athena but didn't find one that I liked. I spent the majority of my time looking at baby things and ended up buying some clothes for Athena. My last stop was the grocery store, where I enjoyed shopping at most. I was in high spirits and was looking forward to getting back to the kids and cooking dinner. I just loved Mom's kitchen. I'd crack open the window just a bit to let some cold air in while cooking. The nippy temperature made it comfortable to make soups and stews unlike back home where it was always hot cooking over the stove. Of all the things I was going to miss the most about being here, it was the weather.

Athena Falls Ill

Not more than an hour after I got back, Athena started to cry like she did the day before, only this time, it was different, more intense. Jessica and I were now both feeling nervous, and I again looked through our discharge papers and found the number to Stanford. With my hands shaking, I pressed the telephone numbers of the hospital on my cell phone and was connected to the cardiology department, then to the physician on call there. She asked me some questions about Athena then told us to take her temperature. She didn't feel hot to the touch, and so we hadn't thought about taking it. As I remained on the phone Jessica held the thermometer under her arm and read it out loud to me after a couple of minutes. She said it was 94 degrees, and we wondered if the thermometer was working right. The doctor said it would be best to take her in to the closet hospital to have her checked. I anxiously tried calling my brother Jimmy several times to ask what hospital to take her to but he didn't answer his phone as he was working. Jessica whisked Athena in her arms, wrapping her in a blanket, and with a sense of urgency, held her in the car, not placing her in her car seat. We punched in the name "hospital" into my GPS and when we arrived at that destination several minutes later; we found it to be a closed behavioral hospital. I asked CJ to call 911 to ask where the closest hospital was. We were told that the nearest one was several minutes away. They asked if we needed an ambulance, but I did not want to wait. I drove as fast as I could; nervously knowing Athena was out of her car seat. She wasn't crying any longer but we still had the innate feeling that something was very wrong.

I dropped CJ, Jessica and the baby off at the front of the facility and nervously parked my car. When I entered the waiting room of the emergency department, I saw that it was packed with people. My daughter was standing at the front desk, with Athena in her arms, while the receptionist asked her a host of questions. When I tried to interrupt her, she said that Athena needed to be assigned a medical record number before they could treat her. I told her with a sense of urgency and a commanding tone to my voice that this baby just had heart surgery a few weeks before and that Stanford believed that she needed to be seen immediately. The receptionist told me to calm down and after her paperwork was completed, she walked them over to triage, which was just a little cubical in the waiting room area. As I tried to walk over there with them I was told that only the parents were allowed there. I didn't want to make a scene for Jessica's sake and restlessly stayed put. When Jessica stepped out of the cubicle she told me they took Athena's temperature under her arm, and when she asked the nurse what it was, she was told 92 degrees. The reading distressed Jessica and she questioned the nurse about it. She was nonchalantly told that temperatures, when taken rectally, were usually two degrees higher. There was no indication that Athena was considered a medical emergency at this point and certainly not treated as one.

After she was assessed at triage, Jess and CJ were led back into the secured emergency room area by a security guard. I was again told that I could not go with them. In my most self-contained state of anger, I explained to the guard that I had come to California to be an advocate for my daughter and CJ, who was a minor at the time and it was unacceptable that I couldn't go in with them. He apologized, but I was still stopped from entering. Not long afterward, I was approached by a female staff member who said because of our circumstances they would make an exception to their policy and let me in. That was a good decision on their part, as I wouldn't have stood for it.

When I entered the room, Athena was awake and lying on

an adult bed with Jessica's hands securing her. She looked so incredibly small on that large gurney. The only person that was in the room besides Jessica and CJ, was a young male nurse, dressed in blue scrubs, who looked like a high school student. He took Athena's temperature rectally, and after he read it he looked confused and left the room. Jessica looked at me as we overheard him asking someone if this temperature reading "sounded right."

A doctor entered the room shortly afterwards and said to put her blanket back on and that they would take her temperature again in a little while. Here is what I still struggle with when looking back. How could this not have set off a huge alarm with these people? A baby that had open-heart surgery just weeks before and being hypothermic?

I can't recall how many minutes went by before her temperature was again taken with yet the same low temperature reading. After they finished taking it, with her pajamas wide open, I said, "Shouldn't she be covered?" We buttoned her up and wrapped her back in the blanket we brought her in. Yet again, no one seemed distressed by her low temperature.

A chest X-ray was ordered and once again Athena was removed from her clothing and X-rays were taken right on the bed, which took quite a while. Leads were put on her chest to monitor her heart, and her heartbeat was normal. We overheard someone asking for a blood pressure cuff, but it appeared they didn't have one for an infant and there was some confusion about finding one. I can't remember when her blood pressure was finally taken or even if it was.

About an hour later, a doctor of pediatric medicine came into the room. I told him that I had brought all of Athena's records from Stanford with us and gave him the several folders that contained all of her medical records. He talked about doing a spinal tap and asked Jessica for permission to do the procedure.

In the interim, we were told that they were in contact with Stanford and that they would be sending a helicopter to medevac her back there.

The doctor who seemed to have taken over her care then ordered an IV and multiple attempts were made to get a line in her. After several failed attempts of trying to get it in a nurse from the pediatric department was summoned for help. She seemed irritated by the other nurses while asking for things that she needed, and she made numerous calls to other departments asking for them. At one point I heard her saying, "I'll just go look for it myself." Soon after we began to see the urgency of what was happening, and the staff there seemed like they were not prepared to handle Athena's medical emergency. We observed nurses and other people running around, looking for things through drawers in the hallway, down the hallway, and in the room itself.

About 45 minutes later, they called for a warmer to place Athena in. Once she was placed in the warmer, another part of the heater was called for, some type of chemical blanket to put underneath her which didn't arrive for yet another ten to fifteen minutes. At this time, they were still trying to get an IV into Athena.

At some point an anesthesiologist was called to help get the line in her. It was obvious that Athena's condition was worsening, as the room was now packed with so many people we were asked to step outside to make room for them.

Jess and CJ remained seated down the hallway while I stood right outside her room watching what was going on. Horrified, I now saw chest compressions being performed on Athena's tiny little body. Not long after, another doctor from the ER emerged from the room and walked up so close to me, our faces almost touched. In almost a whisper he told me," It didn't look good." The next time I spoke to him I asked that if Athena survived, if she would have brain damage to which he replied, "Probably so."

I walked into the room and stood there in shock while they continued with the chest compressions. Her color was gone, and I couldn't believe that this baby, who was alert and alive when we brought her in, was leaving us.

I walked back out of the room so numb I couldn't feel the floor beneath me. I looked at Jessica and CJ sitting there and could barely breathe knowing that in just a matter of minutes their lives would change forever. The innocence of their eighth-grade love, the divine miracle of bringing a child into this world, standing strong and growing closer through the adversity of her heart surgery and recovery. Realizing that the love they felt for each other was small in comparison to the love they now felt for this new little life. The promise of a future with their daughter together.

And then she was gone.

I sat there frozen as the doctor told my daughter that they did everything they could do but that they couldn't save her, that she had died.

In that moment I would have given my life to spare my daughter from the piercing pain of those words. This was my daughter, my child whom I did everything I could to protect since the moment she was born. And there I sat, having to listen to someone tell her that her child had passed away. Please dear God, PLEASE let me wake up. This can't be happening.

At that moment, I was swept into darkness, into a blinding catastrophic storm, and the debris of images went screaming through my head–

"I'm pregnant." "Are you going to tell him?" "I feel the baby moving." "Something is wrong." "Transposition of the Great Arteries." "Surgery in California." "Why Jessica?" "Looks like a girl." "Athena's heartbeat." "Preparing for our trip." "Feeling Athena kick for the first time." "Jessica's photo shoot." "Long, beautiful Hawaiian hair." "The New Little Princess." "Athena's song." "Her baby shower." "Honey, you look so beautiful, you are going to make all the young girls want to become pregnant." "Premature contractions, hospitalization." "Fetal monitors." "Jessica on bed rest." "Shipping my car." "Suitcases packed." "Time to leave." "Goodbye Zoë." "Contractions on the plane." "Touching down." "We're here!" "Limo ride." "Mom's smile the night we arrived." "Steve driving us to Matson." "Picking up my car."

"Our first trip to Stanford." "Driving on the freeways." "The voice of our GPS." "Sightseeing at the Golden Gate Bridge." "Carving Pumpkins." "Fear of bridges." "Arboretum Road." "Meeting her surgeon." "99 percent success rate." "Moving into the Ronald McDonald House." "I think I'm in labor." "Driving to the hospital." "Five centimeters dilated." "The epidural." "Sleeping through labor." "NIC team setting up." "Jessica fully dilated." "Little crop of dark hair." "Her head is out!" "Baptized by her amniotic fluid." "Athena is BORN!" "NIC Team whisking her away." "First visit in the NIC unit." "Praying before her surgery." "Waiting during her surgery." "Surgery went well." "Lines and tubes everywhere." "Jessica frozen in fear." "Athena off the ventilator." "Jessica holding Athena for the first time." "Mother and daughter at last." "JOY." "Moving to Three West." "Released from the hospital on Thanksgiving Day." "Athena in her bassinet at the Ronald McDonald House." "Singing to Athena." "I'll love you forever book." "Completely discharged from the hospital." "Traveling back to Vallejo." "Home at mom's." "Clinking our glasses in celebration." "She's ours now." "Relaxing before our trip back to Hawaii." "Athena in her new swing." "Getting ready to give her a tub bath." "Buying baby clothes." "Our Saturday morning together."

Then, the cover of her book, the story of Athena's 24 days of life, closed.

It has taken me over a year and a half to bring myself to write about her death. I would start to write then stop for weeks and even months at a time. Every time I thought I could muster up the courage to write the last chapter, I'd open my document, stare at the computer screen, and quickly close it in tears. But I can't do this any longer. Either I had to stop writing this memoir altogether or force myself to continue.

But I can't let go of this story, as it is my tribute to my granddaughter, Athena Marie Noelani Lee Kealoha Ramie Reed, a beautiful, living, breathing child of God who graced us with her presence. Who we were privileged to have and love for 24 earthly days. Whose life mattered. Who was loved and grieved by our family, some who met her and most that never did.

I will exclude most of the details of what happened after that night as the days that followed were crushing. I honestly don't even know how we survived them. Having to see my daughter and CJ walk away from their child in that emergency room, taking that one last look at her body before we left was grief beyond measure, despair beyond words.

The emergency room did not have cell phone reception, and we were unable to call anyone while we were struggling there. My husband was out shopping for bassinets, and was just on his way home with the one he had purchased only minutes before I called him to tell him that Athena died. He was only a block from the store, and in a complete state of shock, he turned around and returned it.

Ron, Matt, Kendra, and CJ's mom, immediately flew to California to be with us. Ten days later after making all of the necessary arrangements, we had to return home to Hawaii. As the wheels of the plane touched off the runway I looked at my daughter sitting in her seat, looking straight ahead in silence, and wondered how she would be able to live through this, how she would ever be able to return home without her baby. We were unable bring Athena's body on the same plane as ours due to logistics. But looking back, I believe that it was a blessing in disguise. I don't know how we could have endured knowing that she was below us, when she should have been in Jessica's arms.

Once home and while the rest of the world was preparing for Christmas, we were planning a funeral. My husband, who has put lights up outside of our home every year since our children were young, took them down before he flew back to California.

After we returned home, and after much deliberation, we decided to put up our tree, in memory of Athena. Instead of our traditional 1500 white lights and more than 500 festive ornaments, many of them with our children's pictures when they were little, we only hung the muted gold and silver ornaments, and those of angel figures. There were no gifts to buy. We were paralyzed with sorrow.

After the Christmas season was over, we celebrated her life in the little chapel of the Christian school that both Jessica and her sister attended, where she and CJ met, with their principal and pastor, Mr. Goodale, commemorating the service. It was an intimate, beautiful ceremony that never should have been. Only the shock we were still operating in, allowed us to get through the day.

Her spirit is now cradled in the arms of her Heavenly Father while her body rests in Hawaiian Memorial Park, which you can see from the rear deck of Jessica's bedroom. When we first moved into our house all those years ago, I was slightly bothered with the cemetery being so close by but it didn't last long. The enchanted acres of this property are tucked in below a magnificent mountain range that makes you realize how very small you are and how big God really is. There, you often see sunlight breaking through the clouds, projecting rays down into the park, almost beckoning one up into heaven. In these holy grounds you know, without a shadow of a doubt, that there is a Creator. In years past, for exercise I have walked the cemetery and rode my bike through it. Never in my wildest of imagination did I ever think a granddaughter of mine would be buried in it. If anyone should have been there, it should have been me or my husband but not her.

Christmas will soon be here once again, and we will have a new ornament to hang on the Christmas tree this year, alongside of Athena's.

Legacy, a healthy baby girl, was born to Jessica and CJ on August 31, twenty months after Athena was born. Incredibly, she was born with a birthmark that Jessica swears is in the shape of an angel on the inside of her forearm. I'd like to think that our angel Athena kissed her before she was born so that she's be reminded of her sister who came before her and who will love her forever from afar. The sister she will never know but who she will learn about through pictures and stories. Maybe one day, she'll even read this one.

I once heard a saying that a mother is only as happy as her saddest child. Although Jessica is happy with the birth of Legacy, that broken place in her heart where Athena lives always will be there. She has done most of her grieving in private and has kept a brave front for everyone around her, mainly me. As strong as I tried to be for my daughter throughout all of those months, I just couldn't contain my feelings any longer. I was broken. I felt ashamed of myself for not being able to be stronger for her but I had nothing left to give. I was empty. Jessica lost her child and in a sense, I lost a part of mine, too.

When I look at Jessica now, I don't see that lighthearted, adventurous, giggly little girl any longer. I now see a grown woman, mature beyond her years. The mother of a daughter whom she fought so hard for, who did everything right for. The one who gave me the precious gift of a granddaughter whom I will carry in my heart and love forever.

As I bring this story to a close, I find it amazing that my final words are being typed the day before Athena's would have been two years old. Jessica and I have been preparing for this day by buying beautiful little birthday trinkets to decorate her grave with. Today, I cut the grass and polished her headstone while Jessica and her best friend Melly, placed a birthday banner, a "2" candle and garland along the borders of her grave. Tomorrow, we will bring balloons there, sing Happy Birthday and release them to her in Heaven.

As we come to terms with a loss we will never understand, we are comforted by the gift she gave to us. A love so big and so beautiful it feels like we can hardly contain it. An eternal branch of our family tree, a love that will last forever – our Athena Marie.

Afterword

After Athena died so unexpectedly we were left with the overwhelming task of trying to find out exactly what had happened.

"Why would God bring Athena through her heart surgery, only for her to die from something else?" Jessica cried. Being unable to answer her, I set out on a mission, giving her my word that I would find out.

Stanford brought Athena's tiny little body back to their facility to conduct an autopsy. The report stated that her heart was intact and functioning properly. There appeared to be early signs of pneumonia developing in her left lung but there was no conclusive cause of death explaining what she died from. I couldn't let my daughter spend the rest of her life not knowing and so I spent the better part of the following year trying to fulfill that promise which was long and painful. The anger and grief that consumed me kept me going – literally spending every spare moment I had writing letters, making telephone calls, obtaining records and combing thought all the information I could get my hands on.

Knowing that this was more than I could handle on my own I sought the assistance of an attorney in California who hired a medical expert to examine the records of the hospital that we brought her to that night. There wasn't enough evidence to find the facility negligent although I believe they made numerous errors. Looking back on how they handled Athena's care seemed obvious to me – they didn't react quickly enough to her emergency and weren't prepared to manage it. If they would have placed her on a warmer the moment she was brought in and had a pediatric doctor of medicine see her from the start, maybe its wishful thinking, but I believe she may have lived.

The expert reported that there were questionable areas of her care but it would be an uphill battle to prove the hospital responsible for her death and most likely no attorney in the state of California would take the case due to their tort reform laws. How could we just leave it at this after everything Jessica had been through – and what Athena went through? How could we go on not ever knowing? If it wasn't her heart, then what was it?

I have been able to accomplish most everything that I have set out to do in life and I don't give up easily. But in light of everything I did, and the countless hours spent trying to find that answer for my daughter, I hit a dead end and there was nothing else I could do. I felt that I had failed her and was devastated.

After Athena's funeral we went through the motions of our daily lives but nothing was remotely the same. Our home that was supposed to echo with the sounds of a baby was quieted in sorrow. Her room remained empty and her closet, filled to the brim with clothing, toys and gifts, went untouched.

For the first year, Jessica would rarely talk about Athena and when she would see me cry she'd get upset and say STOP crying." It was hard not being able to talk to her. No one could possibly understand the enormity of what we had been through – what we were going through – besides her, CJ and me. But this is how she coped with her daughter's death and I had to respect her feelings. Knowing that she was suffering behind her bedroom door and not being able to help her, was unbearable.

It was never my intention to write a book, but I found myself on my computer, late at night, when there was nowhere else to turn with the gripping grief I felt. I don't even remember typing most of the story – it just happened. Some nights, I'd manage to get out a few sentences. Others, I'd open my document and just sit there and cry. I often described her death like climbing the largest mountain in the world, then standing at the top waving your trophy in victory, when someone comes along and slaps it out of your hands. Athena was our trophy and she was supposed to be here with us.

I am grateful that Jessica had been the adventurous girl that she was, went to the Christian school she attended, and learned the survival skills she did at the summer camp she went to when she was younger. I believe that the foundation of all of her experiences as a child tethered with the love of her family and friends helped her survive her devastating loss. Her strength was amazing to witness and most of the time, she seemed stronger than the rest of us.

When Athena was to have turned a year old we had a birthday party for her at a beautiful beach park in Kailua, Hawaii. The all-day event was filled with food and music, family and friends. Jessica had a birthday cake made with pictures of her, Athena and CJ printed on the icing. We wrote personal messages on balloons and let them go in unison as we sang Happy Birthday. It was painful yet incredibly spiritual.

About a month after we celebrated Athena's first birthday, Jessica told me that she was pregnant. I think I was more shocked this time than the last but I knew this is what she needed to do. It was hard being happy for her while grieving Athena, but I had to honor her feelings and support the choice she made to become pregnant once again.

Because of Athena's rare heart condition, her new pregnancy was closely monitored and I was on edge once more. On the day Dr. Hirata confirmed that all was well with the baby's heart and that it was a little girl, Jessica and I wept.

Legacy Kamakanamakamaemaikalani Ramie Reed was born on August 31, 2012. Watching her come into our fragile lives was bittersweet. As crazy as it sounds, I was worried that because she was a girl, I would be looking for Athena all over again. Incredibly, Legacy was born with blue eyes unlike Athena's dark brown ones. Both CJ and Jess have brown eyes, and so her eye color was a surprise. I believe that God gave her blue eyes so that she would have her own distinct identity and not have to walk in the shadow of her sister.

My sister Gloria bought Jessica a little memorial figurine of a beautiful ceramic angel with its wings surrounding a photo of Athena. When Legacy started to crawl, Jessica placed it on the bottom shelf of a bookcase that holds our family pictures. Legacy crawls to the picture every morning and has learned to 'kiss sissy'. Jessica keeps Athena close to her in all that she does and takes Legacy to visit her sister's resting place often.

Just recently, while Jessica and I were walking away from Athena's grave, my eyes welled with tears. Instead of saying, STOP crying, Jessica, with Legacy in her arms, tenderly whispered, "Don't cry Mom." Only since Legacy's birth has she been able to fully open up about Athena's death. Now that she has – the healing of our hearts has finally begun.

As painful as it was going through this journey with Jessica – having Athena for those 24 beautiful days was worth every single one of them. I know without a doubt, we'd go through it all over again, just to hold her one last time.

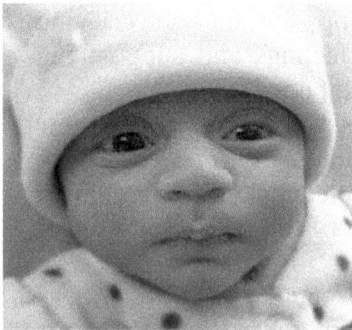

Athena Marie

About the Author

Carol Lee Ramie is a devoted wife and mother of three children, two step children, ten grandchildren and one angel. She lives in a tropical home, nestled near a beautiful mountain range on the Windward side of Oahu, Hawaii where she loves to entertain family and friends. She and her husband have led one of Hawaii's top private investigative firms in the State of Hawaii for the last 33 years, specializing in insurance fraud. Her self-proclaimed passion is the water and swims several miles a week at their local district pool. She is a lover of lyrics and has written and produced songs for her children, grandchildren and friends. Carol has written light hearted family related articles for the column, The Goddess Speaks in their local newspaper. She has a heart of justice, demonstrating remarkable enthusiasm and stamina when helping family and friends during their times of need. She is currently helping to raise the newest addition of the family, her granddaughter Legacy, and plans to write her first children's book soon.